王陆807
雅思词汇
精讲 口语篇
IELTS

王陆 高玉臻 车玲 刘洋 / 编著

第2版

机械工业出版社
CHINA MACHINE PRESS

本书是一部以讲解雅思口语核心词汇为线索的书。全书按照主题进行分类。

拓展词汇部分分为两类：选记词汇和必备词汇。这两种编排能够迅速降低学生的复习工作量，同时提高复习效果。

本书的作者是雅思培训行业权威口语主讲，经验丰富，深受学生喜爱。本书的部分内容一直位于无忧雅思网下载排行榜的前列。

本书是雅思考生口语冲刺的必备图书。

本书繁体中文版已授权台湾博识图书出版有限公司正式出版。

图书在版编目（CIP）数据

王陆807雅思词汇精讲. 口语篇/王陆等编著.—2版.—北京：机械工业出版社，2009.2（2013.11重印）

ISBN 978-7-111-22686-4

I. 王… II. 王… III. ①英语—词汇—高等教育—自学参考资料 ②英语—口语—高等教育—自学参考资料 IV. H313

中国版本图书馆CIP数据核字（2009）第013805号

机械工业出版社（北京市百万庄大街22号 邮政编码 100037）

策划编辑：孟玉琴　　责任编辑：张芳　　版式设计：美文苑

保定市中画美凯印刷有限公司印刷

2013年11月第2版第19次印刷

140mm×203mm・5.375印张・140千字

63 001-68 000册

标准书号：ISBN 978-7-111-22686-4

ISBN 978-7-89482-428-8（光盘）

定价：20.00元（附赠1MP3光盘）

凡购本书，如有缺页、倒页、脱页，由本社发行部调换

电话服务

社服务中心：(010)88361066

销售一部：(010)68326294

销售二部：(010)88379649

读者购书热线：(010)88379203

网络服务

门户网：http://www.cmpbook.com

教材网：http://www.cmpedu.com

一书震雅思

雅思没有词汇表，但是雅思学生常常被拦在词汇关面前。

4年前，王陆第一次给学生讲授听力词汇表，一个学生凭着她的词汇表参加雅思考试，听力得到了7分。那个学生对王陆说："Hallie，我数了一下你的词汇，一共是807个，就叫807词汇吧。"这就是807的来历。4年后，807经过翻新和发展，已经涉及听、说、读、写四个方面，成为了雅思教学的里程碑。

807为我们带来了什么？带来了雅思教学的革命。

807首次强调雅思核心词，强调"张纲举目"的词汇概念。这秉承了王陆教学一贯精炼的风格。通过掌握核心词，扫除词汇在考试中的障碍，达到适应考试的目的。这些核心词是根据历年雅思考试真题，同时结合学生的反馈总结而成的，具有非常强的实战性。因为单词数量有限，所以学生也能够快速掌握。

807进一步强化听、说、读、写的教学特点，这是王陆实战性教学的具体化。在她看来，不同的测试项目有不同的训练目的和方法。听力词汇要求学生能够准确朗读，快速反应，正确拼写。因此，听力书中列举了易混淆词和核心词不同形式的读音、雅思考试中的常见错误和真题中的各类场景；口语词汇要求学生能够正确朗读，并强调选记词汇，做到有的放矢；阅读词汇强调识读，因此可在掌握核心词的基础上通过词汇记忆法，进一步扩充词汇量；写作强调正确拼写和正确使用，所以不仅有单词讲解，而且有拓展词组和例句。

807不仅仅是词汇书，也是机经和答案的结合。这贯穿了王陆高效学习的教学理念。由于书中的所有素材都来自雅思考试，并且配合答案，学生背单词的过程就是全方位复习考试的过程。

就是这样一套书，让众说纷纭的记忆法平息了下来，因为这套书用最简洁和直接的方式解决了沉重的单词负担，缩短了漫长的复习过程！

就是这样一套书，在无忧雅思网的下载榜上，几年来一直名列前茅。无数人在找，无数人在学。在它问世的当天就已经注定了它的不平凡。

我和王陆是亲密无间的合作伙伴，也是无话不谈的真挚朋友。她是一个不断进取的人，看到她每年一个台阶一个台阶地进步，我感到无比喜悦和骄傲！感谢她给我这样一个机会，仅以此文代序。

吕 蕾

王陆的道与807的根

任何一个人都是不平凡的，假如他/她的生活充满了向上的内容。王陆就是这样的一个能人。

对于IELTS考试来说，王陆象征着权威。从王陆将无限的个人激情投入到英语教学的那天起，中国的IELTS考试中就出现了一个特别的师者，虽然中国的IELTS教学中从来不缺少师者。然而师者与师者是不同的。有的师者象征着一种学术造诣的深厚，有的师者是因为他们可以掀起一场场的创新。王陆的师者内涵二者皆有。

对于学生，她不仅授之以知识，更有智慧；对于学术，她不仅待之以认真，更有创新。在众多的创新中，807词汇是最具意味的一个。

对于IELTS听力来说，807意味着精华。从王陆将无数的听力词汇凝练为807个单词的那天起，中国的IELTS考试中就出现了一个冠顶的奇迹，虽然中国的IELTS教学中从来不缺少奇迹。然而奇迹与奇迹是不同的。有的奇迹意味着一种无可超越的巅峰，有的奇迹是因为它们可以引发一连串的奇迹。王陆的807词汇兼顾二者。

国内的IELTS听力教学法是有它的进化论的。从最初的场景教学法，到后来的定位听力法，中国的师者一直在探寻升腾。最初的807词汇在众多名师的眼睛里是微不足道的，因为大家都不相信这薄薄的小册子在繁杂的IELTS听力考试面前能有何作用。然而，中国考生IELTS听力成绩的大幅提高最终证明了一切！

不求名、不求虚，唯求实是王陆的道！不求高、不求深，只求用就是807的根。

最初的807听力只有一本书，后来吕蕾女士建议以同样的思维开发阅读、口语和写作，成就了今天一套完整的807词汇。

这是一项浩大的工程，饱含了很多人的心血！在本书的编写过程中，我、刘洋、马龙、车玲、裘杨、马俊哲、李炳军、钟一、刘钰、李国禧、Emily、郭小婉、厉洁、满金麒、宋丽、牛振芳、程云云、张靖娴、蒋庆华也参与了资料收集及部分编写工作，在此一并致谢。

马 良

目录

acrobatics 杂技

选 记 杂技 acrobatics [ˌækrəˈbætɪks] *n.*
杂技演员 acrobat [ˈækrəbæt] *n.*
杂技团团员 trouper [ˈtruːpə] *n.*
杂技场 acrobatic theatre
杂技艺术 acrobatic art
现代杂技 modern acrobatics
民间杂技 folk acrobatics
杂技比赛 acrobatic competition
杂技节 acrobatic festival
杂技团 acrobatic troupe

adventure 冒险

Tips: 适用于 an adventurous person (一个冒险的人)。

必 备 冒失鬼 daredevil [ˈdeədevl] *n.*
跳伞 skydiving [ˈskaɪdaɪvɪŋ] *n.*
危险的 dangerous [ˈdeɪndʒərəs] *adj.*
降落伞 parachute [ˈpærəʃuːt] *n.*
羞怯的 timid [ˈtɪmɪd] *adj.*
行为 behavior [bɪˈheɪvjə(r)] *n.*
兴奋的，激动的 thrilling [ˈθrɪlɪŋ] *adj.*
爱冒险的人 adventurous person
冒险家 risk-takers
热气球 hot-air balloon
跳伞运动员 sky diver
蹦级 bungee jumping
悬挂式滑翔运动 hang-gliding
极限运动 extreme game
赛车 car racing
吉尼斯世界记录 The Guinness Book of World Records

冒险 take risks
恐高 afraid of height
寻求刺激 seek thrills
引发危险 cause danger
有更强的好奇心 have more curiosity
为了刺激而奉献生命 give up life for thrills
迎合一些电视观众的口味 cater to the tastes of some TV viewers
装备和设备 gears or facilities

advertisement 广告

Tips: 适用于 an advertisement (一则广告)。

必备 汽车 automobile ['ɔːtəməbiːl] *n.*
钻石项链 diamond necklace
留下深刻的印象 make a deep impression
记住品牌 remember brand
公益广告 non-profitable ads
提高产品销量 increase sales of products
新品牌 new brand
提高声誉 improve reputation
非盈利的 non-profitable
遵照社会标准 follow social norms
误导消费者 mislead consumers
广告的焦点 focus of ads
损坏信用 ruin the credit
高质量的象征 symbol of high quality
商业广告 commercial advertisement
分类广告 classified advertisement

选记 副刊 supplement ['sʌplɪmənt] *n.*
广告商 advertiser ['ædvətaɪzə] *n.*

媒体 media ['miːdɪə] *n.*

广告招贴画 poster ['pəʊstə] *n.*

广告牌 billboard ['bɪlbɔːd] *n.*

商业广告 commercial [kə'mɜːʃl] *n.*

广告插页 insert [ɪn'sɜːt] *n.*

失物招领启事 lost & found

标志 sign [saɪn] *n.*

登广告 advertising ['ædvətaɪzɪŋ] *n.*

选择性的 alternative [ɔːl'tɜːnətɪv] *adj.*

目录 catalog ['kætəlɒg] *n.*

小册子 brochure ['brəʊʃə(r)] *n.*

飞行员 flyer ['flaɪə] *n.*

宣传 promo ['prəʊməʊ] *n.*

预告片 trailer ['treɪlə(r)] *n.*

宣传 publicity [pʌb'lɪsətɪ] *n.*

标语 slogan ['sləʊgən] *n.*

做广告宣传 advertise ['ædvətaɪz] *v.*

促销 promote [prə'məʊt] *v.*

食物 food [fuːd] *n.*

零食 snack [snæk] *n.*

葡萄酒 wine [waɪn] *n.*

酒精 alcohol ['ælkəhɒl] *n.*

手机 automobile ['ɔːtəməbiːl] *n.*

电视 TV [ˌtiː'viː]

互联网 Internet ['ɪntənet] *n.*

户外的 outdoor ['aʊtdɔː(r)] *adj.*

杂志 magazine [ˌmægə'ziːn] *n.*

报纸 newspaper ['njuːspeɪpə(r)] *n.*

价格 price [praɪs] *n.*

质量 quality ['kwɒlətɪ] *n.*
效果 effect [ɪ'fekt] *n.*
帆布鞋 sneakers ['sniːkəs] *n.*
计算机 computer [kəm'pjuːtə(r)] *n.*
电器 appliance [ə'plaɪən] *n.*
生产 manufacture [ˌmænjʊ'fæktʃə(r)] *v.*
飞机放烟组成的空中文字 skywriting
电视推销 telemarketing ['telɪmɑːkɪtɪŋ] *n.*
商业栏 business section
社论版 editorial page
科技版 science and technology page
体育版 sports section
娱乐版 amusement page
新闻版 news hole
金融版 financial page
社会新闻版 city news
广告版 advertisement page
日发行量 daily circulation
报贩 news vendor
记者招待会 press conference / news conference
发布新闻 publish the news
新闻封锁 news blockout
言论自由 liberty of speech
报纸报道 press coverage
采集新闻 gather news
广告社 advertising agency
广告代理人 advertising agent
在电视上做广告 advertise on TV
社会公益广告 public service advertising

广告妙语 attention-getter
广告片 advertising film
霓虹灯广告 neon-light advertisement
户外广告 outdoor advertising
邮寄广告宣传品 junk mail
浮夸的广告 glossy advertisement
整版广告 full-page advertisement
广告栏 advertisement column
征婚广告 matrimonial notice
结婚启事 marriage announcement
招聘广告 want ads
招聘广告vacant ['veɪkənt] *n.*
雇佣启事 help wanted
出版社 publishing house
来宾留言簿 visitors' book
广告宣传活动 advertising campaign
户外露天大广告牌 outdoor billboards
滚动的板 rolling boards
购买点的传播媒介 point-of-purchase media
停车计时收费器 parking meter
运输广告 transit ads
车站招贴 station posters
消费者信用卡 consumer credit card
产品广告 product advertisement
有营养的食物 nutritional food
直邮 direct mail
播送传播 broadcast media
印刷传播 print media
电子传播 electronic media

提高销量 increase the sales
促销产品 promote the products
获取利润 make a profit
休息 have a rest
提供关于产品信息 provide information about products
使人们得病 make people sick
夸大功能 exaggerate the functions
误导消费者 misguide the consumers
不适合孩子观看的 not suitable for children to watch
引起观众负面情绪 cause the negative mood of audience
高成本 high cost
买广告产品 buy the products advertised
买他们不需要的东西 buy what they don't need
更新他们的动产 update their belongings
消费者的利益 benefits of consumers
产品的功能 functions of products
满足儿童的需求 satisfy the demands of children
买他们孩子喜欢的东西 buy what their children like
使孩子更聪明和健康 make their children more intelligent and healthier
做聪明的选择 make a wise choice
高质量 high quality
运动设施 sports facilities
著名品牌 famous brands
产品质量 quality of product
追求奢华 pursue luxuries

a work of art 艺术品

Tips: 适用于 a work of art (一件艺术品) 和 an old object (一个家中的旧东西)。

必 备 理论 theory ['θɪərɪ] *n.*
天赋 talent ['tælənt] *n.*
艺术展览馆 art gallery
画草图 draw the sketch
激发学生的趣 motivate students' interest
充满想象力 full of imagination
观察物体 observe objects
增值 gain good value
社会地位的象征 symbols of social status
用画来装饰屋子 decorate rooms with painting
花或风景 flowers or landscape
代表社会地位 represent social status
西方画作 western paintings
不同文化和风格 different cultures and styles
教育的一部分 part of education
从本质上鉴别物体 identify objects in nature
花的特质 specific nature of flowers
有天赋的人 gifted people
有更好的审美能力 have better sense of beauty
有观察力 have the skill of observation
忘记烦恼和忧愁 forget their troubles and worries
心态平和 have the peace of mind
理论知识 theoretical knowledge
实践技能 practical skill

beach 海滨

必 备 海滨度假胜地 beach [bi:tʃ] *n.*

海滨服装 beachwear ['biːtʃweə(r)] *n.*
海滨的木板人行道 boardwalk ['bɔːdwɔːk] *n.*
海滨旅馆 beachside hotel
海滨袋 beach bag
海滨浴场 bathing beach
大遮阳伞 beach umbrella

birds 鸟类

Tips: 适用于关于鸟类的问题。

必备 麻雀 sparrow ['spærəʊ] *n.*
燕子 swallow ['swɒləʊ] *n.*
海鸟 seabird ['siːbɜːd] *n.*
鸳鸯 lovebird ['lʌvbɜːd] *n.*
仙鹤 crane [kreɪn] *n.*
鸣禽 songbird ['sɒŋbɜːd] *n.*
稀有鸟类 rare birds
野鸭 wild duck
保护环境 protect the environment
偷鸟蛋是非法的 illegal to take their eggs

birthday 生日

Tips: 适用于 birthday celebration (生日庆祝)。

必备 野餐 barbecue ['bɑːbɪkjuː] *n.*
值得纪念的 memorable ['memərəbl] *adj.*
周年纪念 anniversary [ˌænɪ'vɜːsərɪ] *n.*
生日庆祝会 birthday celebration
庆祝生日 celebrate birthday
烤虾 baked prawns
贝壳 shells [ʃelz] *n.*
篝火晚会 bonfire party
讲故事 tell stories

准备生日蛋糕 prepare a birthday cake
许愿 make a wish
吹蜡烛 blow the candles
分蛋糕 share the cake
唱歌跳舞 sing and dance
聚会 have a get-together
收到礼物 receive gifts
家庭庆典 family ceremony
特殊的聚会 special parties
重要场合 important occasions
表达我们的关注和情感 express our concern and emotions
聊天 chat [tʃæt] *n.*
录像带 video [ˈvɪdɪəʊ] *n.*
告别会 farewell party
回忆珍贵事件 recall precious memory
打牌 play cards
唱歌 sing songs
丰富的正餐 profuse dinner
安排庆祝会 arrange the party
饮料和零食 drinks and snacks
发邀请 send invitations
筹备活动 prepare activities
正式和非正式的晚会 formal and informal party
感到放松 feel relaxed
商业谈判 business negotiation
在外吃饭 dine out
立体声音响 stereo system
记录整个过程 record the whole process
吸引注意 draw attention

玩游戏 play games

book 图书

Tips: 适用于 your favorite book (你最喜爱的书)、a story in your childhood (童年的故事)、a character in film or TV (电影或电视中的人物)。在描述休闲活动、爱好时，可以提及此方面。

必备 趋势 trend [trend] *n.*
个性 individuality [ˌɪndɪˌvɪdjʊ'ælɪtɪ] *n.*
消极的 negative ['negətɪv] *adj.*
不友好的 hostile ['hɒstaɪl] *adj.*
好攻击的 aggressive [ə'gresɪv] *adj.*
模仿 imitate ['ɪmɪteɪt] *v.*
配件 accessories [ək'sesərɪz] *n.*
寓言 fable ['feɪbl] *n.*
娱乐 entertainment [entə'teɪnmənt] *n.*
卡通片 cartoon [kɑː'tuːn] *n.*
英雄主义 heroic deed
照别人的方式去做 follow suit
看卡通片 watch cartoons
受教育 get education
生活哲学 life philosophy
成功的商人 successful businessmen
传统美德 traditional virtues
消极的感受 negative feelings
运动区 sports field
娱乐区 entertainment field
模仿他们的偶像 imitate their idols
买衣服 buy the clothes
娱乐方式 entertainment ways
休闲活动 leisure activities

留下深刻印象 make a deep impression
连环画 comic books
图画书 picture books
复述故事 retell the story
拓宽视野 widen their sights
自然与科学 nature and science
有耐心 have patience
类别 category ['kætəgərɪ] *n.*
传统方式 traditional way
疼痛的眼睛 sore eyes
分享意见 share ideas

building 建筑

Tips: 适用于 a building (建筑)。

必备 娱乐 entertainment [ˌentə'teɪnmənt] *n.*
标准泳池 Olympic-sized swimming pool
网球场 tennis court
篮球场 basketball field
足球场 football pitch
休息区 resting area
足部按摩 foot massage
体形 body shape
休闲活动 leisure activities
身体锻炼 physical exercises
攀岩 go rock-climbing
商业区 shopping mall
有压力的生活 stressful life

选记 桥 bridge [brɪdʒ] *n.*
教堂 church ['tʃɜːtʃ] *n.*
监狱 prison ['prɪzn] *n.*

构造，结构 structure [ˈstrʌktʃə(r)] *n.*

摩天大楼 skyscraper [ˈskaɪskreɪpə(r)] *n.*

平房 bungalow [ˈbʌŋgələʊ] *n.*

别墅 villa [ˈvɪlə] *n.*

复式公寓 duplex [ˈdjuːpleks] *n.*

地标 landmark [ˈlændmɑːk] *n.*

村舍 cottage [ˈkɒtɪdʒ] *n.*

卧房兼起居室 bedsit [ˈbedsɪt] *n.*

砖 brick [brɪk] *n.*

混凝土 concrete [ˈkɒŋkriːt] *n.*

水泥 cement [sɪˈment] *n.*

粘土 clay [kleɪ] *n.*

干草 hay [heɪ] *n.*

宽敞的 spacious [ˈspeɪʃəs] *adj.*

拥挤的 crowded [ˈkraʊdɪd] *adj.*

郊区 suburb [ˈsʌbɜːb] *n.*

栅栏 fence [fens] *n.*

车库 garage [ˈgærɑːʒ] *n.*

小路 path [pɑːθ] *n.*

阳台 balcony [ˈbælkənɪ] *n.*

公寓 flat [flæt] *n.*

公寓 apartment [əˈpɑːtmənt] *n.*

建筑，楼 building [ˈbɪldɪŋ] *n.*

泥，淤泥 mud [mʌd] *n.*

在闹市区 downtown [ˌdaʊˈtaʊ] *adv.*

雕塑 statue [ˈstætjuː] *n.*

注册 registration [ˌredʒɪˈstreɪʃn] *n.*

入学 enrollment [ɪnˈrəʊlmənt] *n.*

健身房 gym [dʒɪm] *n.*

剧院 theater ['θɪətə(r)] *n.*
安全 security [sɪ'kjʊrətɪ] *n.*
声誉 reputation [ˌrepjʊ'teɪʃn] *n.*
现代建筑 modern building
办公楼 office building
内部设施 interior facilities
内部装饰 interior decoration
市中心 city center
半独立房子 semi-detached house
独立的房子 detached house
排房 terraced house
前花园 front garden
前门门铃 front doorbell
名人故居 ancient buildings of famous people
历史遗迹 historical sites
历史事件 historical events
祖先的生活方式 lifestyle of ancestors
日用品 daily necessities
老一代 old generations
不同风格的建筑 buildings in different styles
历史的遗留物 remains of history
鉴赏建筑艺术 appreciate art of construction
维护古建筑 preserve ancient buildings
后代，下一代 later generations
历史的一部分 part of history
名胜 places of interest
去观光 go sightseeing
铭记历史 remember the history
回首过往 recall the past

历史的提示 reminder of history
创造力和想象力 creativity and imagination
历史的象征 symbols of history
娱乐场所 places for recreation
地标建筑 landmark building
行政大楼 administration building
主大厅 main hall
名人书法 calligraphies of famous people
逸事和箴言 anecdotes and mottos
多媒体教室 multi-media classrooms
上网 surf the internet
每日的安排 daily routines
投影仪 OHP
有资格的教师 qualified teachers
教具 study aids
教学辅助 teaching aids
运动设施 sports facilities
建筑外观 appearance of the building
教学规范 standard of teaching
各种活动 various activities
当地社区 local community
当地报纸 local newspaper
电视监视 video surveillance
监控来访者 monitor the visitors
动力技术 dynamic technology
有良好的基础 have a good foundation
抗震 resist the earthquake
现代建筑 modern building
用太阳能 use solar energy

camping 露营

必备 露营园 campground ['kæmpgraʊnd] *n.*

露营 camping ['kæmpɪŋ] *n.*

露营者 camper ['kæmpə(r)] *n.*

野餐 picnic ['pɪknɪk] *n.*

篝火 bonfire ['bɒnfaɪə(r)] *n.*

背包 backpack ['bækpæk] *n.*

帐篷 tent [tent] *n.*

公共露营园 public campground

营利性露营园 commercial campground

睡袋 sleeping bag

铺地防潮布 ground cloth

child 儿童

Tips: 适用于 a child (一个小孩) 、favorite game (最喜爱的游戏) 和 toy (玩具)。

必备 规则 regulation [ˌregjʊ'leɪʃn] *n.*

养家糊口的人 breadwinner ['bredwɪnə] *n.*

主导的 dominant ['dɒmɪnənt] *adj.*

自私的 selfish ['selfɪʃ] *adj.*

祖先 ancestor ['ænsestə(r)] *n.*

习俗 custom ['kʌstəm] *n.*

信念 belief [bɪ'liːf] *n.*

传统 tradition [trə'dɪʃn] *n.*

有美味的食物和零食 have delicious food and snacks

有他们想要的东西 have what they want

有压力 have pressure

担心他们的未来 worry about their future

有很多玩具 have a lot of toys

享受他们的童年 enjoy their childhood

学习各种技能 learn all kinds of skills
尽力在学校取得好的分数 try to get good marks at schools
有家庭作业要做 have homework to do
注重理论学习 focus on the theoretical knowledge
太乏味 too monotonous
以教师为中心的 teacher-centered
不合格的 not qualified
教育质量 quality of education
举例 set an example
物质生活 material life
影响孩子的幸福 affect children's happiness
同其他孩子攀比 compare them with other children
打下坚实基础 lay a solid foundation
实践的技能 practical skills
节省 set aside
父母的责任 responsibility of parents
家庭历史 family history
过去的一代人 past generations
家庭单位 family unit
一代一代 from generation to generation

circus 马戏

选 记 马戏 circus ['sɜːkəs] *n.*
观众 audience ['ɔːdɪəns] *n.*
观众 spectator [spek'teɪtə] *n.*
聚光灯 spotlight ['spɒtlaɪt] *n.*
乐池 bandstand ['bændstænd] *n.*
魔术 magic ['mædʒɪk] *n.*
魔术师 magician [mə'dʒɪʃn] *n.*
小丑 clown [klaʊn] *n.*

宽敞的 spacious ['speɪʃəs] *adj.*
有吸引力的 attractive [ə'træktɪv] *adj.*
产品 product ['prɒdʌkt] *n.*
退款 refund [riː'fʌnd] *n.*
商品 commodity [kə'mɒdətɪ] *n.*
担保，保证 guarantee [ˌgærən'tiː] *n.*
特征 feature ['fiːtʃə(r)] *n.*
买主，购买人 purchaser ['pɜːtʃəsə] *n.*
安全 security [sɪ'kjʊərətɪ] *n.*
马戏场 circus arena
流动马戏团 travelling circus
观众席 spectators' seats
杂技迷 acrobatics fan
吞火魔术师 fire-eater
滑稽表演 comic performance
特技 acrobatic feat
表演杂技 perform acrobatics
驯兽员 animal trainer
驯虎员 tiger tamer
驯狗员 dog trainer
动物表演的节目 animal act
猴戏 monkey show
飞刀演员 knife-thrower

city 城市

Tips: 适用于关于家乡的问题。例如：your favorite city (你最喜爱的城市) 和 a place you would like to visit (你想参观的地方)。

必备 大都市 metropolis [mə'trɒpəlɪs] *n.*
首都 capital ['kæpɪtl] *n.*
风景 landscape ['lændskeɪp] *n.*

迷人的 enchanting [ɪn'tʃɑːntɪŋ] *adj.*
遗迹 remains [rɪ'meɪnz] *n.*
游客 tourist ['tʊərɪst] *n.*
平静的 peaceful ['piːsfl] *adj.*
古都 ancient capital
直辖市 municipality under the central government
沿海城市 coastal city
悠久的历史 long history
现代都市 modern city
省会 provincial capital
古城 ancient city / historical city
偏远城市 remote city
旅游城市 tourist city
古建筑 ancient building
当地人 local people
商业中心 commercial center
文化遗迹 cultural sites
精致的雕塑 exquisite sculpture
宏伟的建筑 magnificent building
景点 scenic spots
当地的食物 local food
当地的景色 local scenery
自然风景 natural landscape
愉快的记忆 happy memories
辛辣食物 spicy food
火锅 hot pot

选记
美食家 gourmet ['gʊəmeɪ] *n.*
渡船 ferry ['ferɪ] *n.*
路标 signpost ['saɪnpəʊst] *n.*

经济 economy [ɪ'kɒnəmɪ] *n.*
文化 culture ['kʌltʃə(r)] *n.*
交通 transport [træn'spɔːt] *v.*
人口 population [ˌpɒpjʊ'leɪʃn] *n.*
地理位置 geographical location
船运商品 shipping goods
传统食物 traditional food
壮丽的风景 splendid scenery
拓宽的马路 broadened street
当地旅游业 local tourism
城市规划 city planning
流动人口 migrating population
历史古迹 historical sites
天然港 natural harbor
人工港 artificial harbor
自由港 free port
海港 coastal port
商港 commercial port

clothes or jewelry 服饰

Tips: 适用于 your favorite clothes or jewelry (最喜爱的服装或珠宝)。

必备 珠宝 jewelry ['dʒuːəlrɪ] *n.*
项链 necklace ['neklɪs] *n.*
手链 bracelet ['breɪslɪt] *n.*
耳环 earrings [ɪə(r)rɪŋz] *n.*
黄金 gold [gəʊld] *n.*
钻石 diamond ['daɪəmənd] *n.*
珠子 bead [biːd] *n.*
胸针 brooch [brəʊtʃ] *n.*

手镯 bangle ['bæŋgl] *n.*
水晶 crystal ['krɪstl] *n.*
时尚 fashion ['fæʃn] *n.*
时髦的 fashionable ['fæʃnəbl] *adj.*
套装 suit [su:t] *n.*
趋势 trend [trend] *n.*
有格调的 stylish ['staɪlɪʃ] *adj.*
精品店 boutique [bu:'ti:k] *n.*
独一无二的 unique [ju:'ni:k] *adj.*
性格 personality [ˌpɜ:sə'nælətɪ] *n.*
兴趣 interest ['ɪntrəst] *n.*
制服 uniform ['ju:nɪfɔ:m] *n.*
职业 occupation [ˌɒkjʊ'peɪʃn] *n.*
个性 individuality [ˌɪndɪˌvɪdʒʊ'ælətɪ] *n.*
休闲服 casual wear
舒适的衣服 comfortable clothes
传统服装 traditional costume
外向的 out-going

选 记 T恤衫 T-shirt
内衣 underclothes ['ʌndəkləʊðz] *n.*
纽扣 button ['bʌtn] *n.*
领带 tie [taɪ] *n.*
领带扣针 tiepin ['taɪpɪn] *n.*
袜子 sock [sɒk] *n.*
长袜 stocking ['stɒkɪŋ] *n.*
围巾 scarf [skɑ:f] *n.*
服装 clothes [kləʊðz] *n.*
服装 clothing ['kləʊðɪŋ] *n.*
服装 costume ['kɒstjʊm] *n.*

服装 dress [dres] *n.*
服装 attire [əˈtaɪə] *n.*
服装 garments [ˈɡɑːmənts] *n.*
服装 apparel [əˈpærəl] *n.*
和服 kimono [kɪˈməʊnəʊ] *n.*
袖子 sleeve [sliːv] *n.*
领子 collar [ˈkɒlə(r)] *n.*
领口 neckline [ˈneklaɪn]*n.*
腰身 waist [weɪst] *n.*
腰围 waistline [ˈweɪstlaɪn] *n.*
风帽 hood [hʊd] *n.*
拉链 zipper [ˈzɪpə] *n.*
凉鞋 sandals [ˈsændlz] *n.*
拖鞋 slippers [ˈslɪpəz] *n.*
鞋跟 heel [hiːl] *n.*
鞋底 sole [səʊl] *n.*
鞋垫 insole [ˈɪnsəʊl] *n.*
羊绒衫 cashmere sweater
丧服 mourning apparel
中装 Chinese-style clothes
便装 casual clothes / casual wear
猎装 hunting costume
马褂 mandarin jacket
中式小褂 Chinese-style shirt
传统服装 traditional garments
民族服装 national costume
男式时装 men's fashion
女式时装 women's fashion
奇异服装 fantastic garments

合身的衣服 fitted clothes
不合身的衣服 ill-fitted clothes
有袖衣服 sleeved garments
无袖衣服 sleeveless garments
定制的服装 made-to-order clothes
机器缝制的衣服 machine-made clothes
手工缝制的衣服 handmade clothes
节日服装 holiday attire
单色衣服 single-coloured clothes
服装式样 dress style
最新款式 latest fashion
时装 fashionable clothes
垫肩 shoulder pad
领扣 collar button
V字领 V-neck
U字领 U-neck
小圆领 Peter Pan collar / Peter pan
船领 boat neck
漆皮鞋 patent-leather shoes
运动鞋 sports shoes
帆布鞋 canvas shoes
网球鞋 tennis shoes
船鞋 step-in
平跟鞋 flat heels
高跟鞋 high heels

club 俱乐部

必备 跳舞俱乐部 dancing club
表达情感 express emotions
分享共同的兴趣 share same interest

吃菜 take some dishes
野餐 have a picnic
去露营 go camping
加入俱乐部 join clubs
垒球俱乐部 baseball clubs
篮球俱乐部 basketball clubs
羽毛球俱乐部 badminton clubs
绘画俱乐部 painting clubs
加入休闲俱乐部 join relaxation clubs
运动俱乐部 sports clubs

collection 搜集品

必备 亲笔签名 autograph ['ɔːtəgrɑːf] *n.* & *v.*
高兴 pleasure ['pleʒə(r)] *n.*
珠宝 jewelry ['dʒuːəlrɪ] *n.*
有耐心 have patience
汽车模型 car model
蝴蝶标本 butterfly specimens
背景知识 background knowledge
成就感 sense of achievement
古币 ancient coins
香水瓶 perfume bottles
绒毛玩具 stuffed animals

color 颜色

Tips: 适用于关于颜色的问题。

必备 红色 red [red] *n.*
激情 passion ['pæʃn] *n.*
绿色 green [griːn] *n.*
和平 peace [piːs] *n.*
能量 energy ['enədʒɪ] *n.*

蓝色 blue [bluː] *n.*
平静的 calm [kɑːm] *adj.*
紫色 purple ['pɜːpl] *n.*
神秘 mystery ['mɪstərɪ] *n.*
黄色 yellow ['jeləʊ] *n.*
皇家的 royal ['rɒɪəl] *adj.*

customs 风俗

必 备 宽容的 tolerant ['tɒlərənt] *adj.*
日常事务 routines [ruː'tiːnz] *n.*
文化差异 cultural differences
当地的语言 local language
文化冲击 cultural shock

dancing 舞蹈

Tips: 适用于关于舞蹈的问题。

必 备 芭蕾舞 ballet ['bæleɪ] *n.*
身体抖动 body shaking
摇摆身体 sway the body
有好身材 have a good figure
特殊训练 special training
手臂动作 arm movement
新疆舞 dance of Xinjiang
二人转 sing and dance duet
钢管舞 pole dance
扇子舞 fan dancing
腰鼓舞 waist drum dance
唐朝舞蹈 dance in Tang Dynasty
街舞 hip-hop
优雅的舞蹈 graceful dance

现代舞 modern dance
民间舞 folk dance
交际舞 ballroom dance
独舞 solo dance
秧歌 yangko dance

选记 伦巴舞 rumba ['rʌmbə] *n.*
桑巴舞 samba ['sæmbə] *n.*
探戈舞 tango ['tæŋgəʊ] *n.*
狐步舞 (四步) foxtrot ['fɒkstrɒt] *n.*
恰恰舞 cha-cha
迪斯科 disco ['dɪskəʊ] *n.*
草裙舞 hula ['hu:lə] *n.*
秧歌队 yangko troupe
化装舞会 fancy ball / costume ball
化装舞会 masque [mɑ:sk] *n.*
慈善舞会 charity dance
贴面舞 cheek dance
踢踏舞 tap dance
草裙 grass skirt
肚皮舞 belly dance
花鼓舞 drum dance
夜总会 night club
舞票 dance coupon
舞伴 dancing partner

economy / business 经济 / 商务

必备 董事会 board of directors
总裁 president / director-general
企业特别助理 special assistant of the enterprise
行政副总裁 administrative deputy president

财务副总裁 financial deputy president
营销中心的沟通职责 the communication responsibility of the marketing center
顾客需求信息 demand information of customers
新产品信息 information of new products
竞争产品情况 situation of compatible products
品种计划 variety plan
市场环境信息 information of the market environment
行业发展情况 developing situation of the industry
市场细分 subdivision of the market
市场定位 market positioning
营销大区 large section of marketing
品牌规划 trademark plan
需求计划 requirements planning
顾客购买习惯 purchasing habits of customers
顾客购买力 purchasing power of customers
顾客满意信息 satisfaction information of customers
订货信息 information of ordering goods
顾客投诉 customers' complaints
营销员培训要求 training request for the marketing employee
经销商培训要求 training request for the distributor
员工素质分析 workers' educational level analysis
研发中心 research and invention center
定型 finalize the design
营销中心 marketing center
生产中心 production center
供应部 supply department
财务部 financial department
业务部 business department

设计处 design division
市场部 market department
广告媒体 advertisement media
广告处 advertisement division
品质部 quality department
储运部 warehousing and transportation department
相关分厂 relevant branch factory
企划部 enterprise planning department
人力资源部 human resources department
监察委 supervision committee
行政部 administrative department
审计部 audit department

electric appliance 电器

Tips: 适用于 equipment (常用的电器)。

必备 洗碗机 dishwasher ['dɪʃwɒʃə(r)] *n.*
电冰箱 fridge [frɪdʒ] *n.*
便携的 portable ['pɔːtəbl] *adj.*
烤面包机 toaster ['təʊstə] *n.*
压榨器 squeezer ['skwiːzə] *n.*
开瓶器 corkscrew ['kɔːkskruː] *n.*
洗衣机 washing machine
电器 electric appliance
洗衣服 wash clothes
省去麻烦 save trouble
真空吸尘器 vacuum cleaners
吸尘器 hoover ['huːvə(r)] *n.*
手机 mobile phone
数码相机 digital camera
智能机器人 intelligent robot

干杂活儿 do chores
电脑科技 computer technology
数码摄像机 digital video camera
排风扇 extractor fan
排油机 smoke exhaust
榨果汁机 juice extractor
搅拌器 food mixer
开罐器 can opener
电动搅拌器 electric mixer
便于操作 easy to operate
插上插头 plug in

选 记 案板 worktop ['wɜːktɒp] *n.*
煮水壶 kettle ['ketl] *n.*
雨伞 umbrella [ʌm'brelə] *n.*
温度计 thermometer [θə'mɒmɪtə(r)] *n.*
电视机 television ['telɪˌvɪʒn] *n.*
电视接收器 TV receiver
电视接收器 tube [tjuːb] *n.*
电源线 power cord
冷冻柜 freezer ['friːzə(r)] *n.*
步行者录放机 walkman ['wɔːkmən] *n.*
放大管 amplifier ['æmplɪfaɪə] *n.*
扬声器 loudspeaker [ˌlaʊd'spiːkə] *n.*
耳机 headphone ['hedfəʊnz] *n.*
耳机 earphone ['ɪəfəʊn] *n.*
电池 battery ['bætərɪ] *n.*
零件 accessory [ək'sesərɪ] *n.*
打蛋器 egg-beater
砧板 chopping board

擀面板 moulding board
玻璃滤壶 pyrex glass
门铃 door bell
钥匙圈 key ring
万能钥匙 master-key
号码锁 combination lock
太阳帽 sun helmet
黑白电视机 black-and-white TV
彩色电视机 colour TV
有线电视 cable TV
闭路电视 closed-circuit TV
显像管 picture tube
电源开关 power switch
音量调节键 sound volume
耳机插孔 earphone jack
使用说明书 operation manual
多制式 multi-system
显示时钟 display clock
标准程序 normal cycle
单独洗衣 wash only
排水钮 drain button
脱水钮 spin button
漂洗钮 rinse button
干洗 dry-cleaning
排水管 water discharge pipe / water outlet
制冰盘 ice tray
蔬菜柜 vegetable crisper
蛋架 egg pocket
柜内灯 interior lamp

室内空气调节器 room air conditioner
遥控器 remote control
操作显示屏 operation display
暖气运转 heating operation mode
冷气运动 cooling operation mode
电唱机 electric gramophone
汽车收音机 auto radio
录音机 tape recorder
卡式录音机 cassette recorder
手提式录音机 portable recorder
对讲机 intercommunication phone
电磁炉 electomagnetic oven
微波炉 microwave oven
电扇 electric fan
电热器 electric heater
电动剃须刀 electric shaver
电视摄像机 TV camera
电源转换器 AD adapter
太阳能电池 solar battery
短路 short circuit

entertainment 娱乐

必备 舞厅 dance hall
划船 rowing ['rəʊɪŋ] *n.*
游艇 yacht [jɒt] *n.*
打猎 hunting ['hʌntɪŋ] *n.*
放风筝 kite flying
秋千 swing [swɪŋ] *n.*
套圈 quoits [kwɔɪts] *n.*
娱乐场 amusement arcade

娱乐厅 pleasure-house
舞池 dance floor
游园会 garden entertainment
露天游乐场 fun fair
公共露天游乐场 amusement park
游船 pleasure boat
打靶 target practice
玩跷跷板 play at seesaw
跳绳 rope skipping
旋转木马 merry-go-round
旋转飞椅 chair o'plane
过山车 roller coaster
观景小铁路 scenic railway
荡秋千 play on a swing
测力机 try-your-strength machine
老虎机 slot machine
碰碰车 bumper car
哈哈镜室 room with distorting mirrors

environment 环境

Tips：适用于 environment in one's hometown (家乡的环境)，描述家乡、城市时，可以谈论这个方面。

必备 居民 inhabitant [ɪn'hæbɪtənt] *n.*
现象 phenomenon [fə'nɒmɪnən] *n.*
生物公害 biohazards [ˌbaɪəʊ'hæzədz] *n.*
污染 pollute [pə'luːt] *v.*
污染 contaminate [kən'tæmɪneɪt] *v.*
污染 pollution [pə'luːʃn] *n.*
污染 contamination [kənˌtæmɪ'neɪʃn] *n.*
空气污染 air pollution

工业城市 industrial city
主要来源 main source
尾气 exhaust gas
温室效应 greenhouse effect
严重的头痛 serious headache
改进技术 improve technology
呼吸新鲜空气 enjoy fresh air
现代工业 modern industry
污染水 pollute water
吸入空气 inhale air
做出限制 make a restriction
检查工厂 examine factories
污染环境 pollute the environment
解决污染问题 solve the pollution problem
政府的责任 responsibility of government
大问题 big issue
环境保护 environmental protection
工业公害 industrial nuisance
有毒气体 poisonous gas
有毒化学品 poisonous chemicals
臭氧层 ozone layer
核污染 nuclear contamination
核辐射 nuclear radiation
核废料 nuclear waste
核材料 nuclear material
核试验 nuclear test
核电厂 nuclear power plant
环境污染物 environmental pollutant

family member 家人

Tips: 适用于 a past family member (过世的家庭成员) 和 two people in the same family (一家里的两口人)。

必备 收入 income [ˈɪŋkʌm] *n.*
地位 status [ˈsteɪtəs] *n.*
社会的象征 symbol of society
离婚率 divorce rate
经济形势 economic situation
溺爱孩子 spoil children
管教孩子 discipline the children
敬老 respect the old
代沟 generation gap
生活水平 living standard

famous person 名人

必备 偶像 idol [ˈaɪdl] *n.*
赚钱 make a lot of money
受到尊敬 be respected by others
有成就感 have the sense of achievement
满足虚荣心 vanity can be satisfied
过奢华的生活 enjoy luxurious life
拥有特权 have some privileges
生命处于危险中 life is in danger
失去自由、隐私 lose freedom / privacy
有压力 have a lot of pressure
关注公众形象 care about your public image
误导消费者 mislead the consumers
影响形象 ruin their image

favorite way of communication 交流方式

Tips: 适用于 your favorite way of communication (最喜爱的交流方式)。

必备 聊天 chat [tʃæt] *n.*

发达的技术 developed technology

分享感受 share the feeling

分享美丽 share the beauty

对……有益 be beneficial to

手机 mobile phones

打电话 make a telephone call

发短信 send SMS

博客留言 leave messege at the blog

发邮件 send emails

写信 write letters

festival 节日

Tips: 适用于 traditional event (一次传统事件) 和 happy event (快乐事件)。

必备 庆典礼仪 celebration [ˌselɪ'breɪʃn] *n.*

鞭炮 firecracker ['faɪəˌkrækə] *n.*

焰火 firework ['faɪəwɜːk] *n.*

磕头 kowtow [ˌkaʊ'taʊ] *v.*

灯笼 lantern ['læntən] *n.*

传说 legend ['ledʒənd] *n.*

庆祝会 celebration [ˌselɪ'breɪʃn] *n.*

权利 power ['paʊə(r)] *n.*

愤怒 passion ['pæʃn] *n.*

阐明 illustrate ['ɪləstreɪt] *v.*

成熟 maturity [mə'tjʊərətɪ] *n.*

保证 guarantee [ˌgærən'tiː] *n.*

瀑布 waterfall ['wɔːtə(r)fɔːl] *n.*
压力 pressure ['preʃə(r)] *n.*
振奋的 refreshed [rɪ'freʃd] *adj.*
四季节庆 holidays and festivals
元旦 New Year's Day
春节 Spring Festival
过年 celebrate the New Year
除夕 New Year's Eve
守岁 stay up all night on Lunar New Year's Eve
年夜饭 feast on the Eve of the Spring Festival
拜年 pay a New Year call
吃饺子 have jiao-zi
团圆 family reunion
年糕 New Year cake
春卷 spring roll
祭祖 hold a memorial ceremony for ancestors
祖宗牌位 memorial tablet
年货 food for the Spring Festival
春联 Spring Festival couplets
迎春晚会 evening party celebrating the Spring Festival
春节联欢 gala celebration for the Spring Festival
压岁钱 lucky money
元宵节 Lantern Festival
传统节日 traditional festivals
家庭团聚 family reunion
有力的家族关系 strong family ties
中国阴历 Chinese lunar calendar
一起吃饭 have dinner together
有新鲜水果 have fresh fruit

庆祝节日 celebrate festival
永恒的生命 eternal life
纪念 in honor of
龙舟节 Dragon Boat Festival
生活水准 living standard
庆祝快乐的事件 celebrate happy events
好身体 good health
美味的食物 delicious food
成功的职业生涯 successful career
性格魅力 charm of personality
奉献精神 spirit of devotion
理性意识 rational sense
快乐的标准 standard of happiness
完美的假期 perfect holiday
导游 tour guide
自然的魔力 magic of nature
水流倾泻 roar of the water
去电影院 go to cinemas
喝茶 have tea
美味的饭食 delicious meals
拍照片 take photos
谈话 have some talk
参加生日庆祝会 attend the birthday celebrations
奢华的庆祝 luxurious celebration
炫耀 show off

选 记 花灯 festive lantern
踩高跷 walk on stilts
赶庙会 go to the fair
扫墓 pay a visit to a tomb

祭品 sacrificial offerings
粽子 pyramid-shaped dumpling
狮子舞 lion dance
赛龙舟 dragon-boat racing
中秋节 Mid-Autumn Festival
月饼 moon cake
赏月 enjoy the full moon
国庆节 National Day
国庆晚会 evening party celebrating National Day
国庆盛典 grand ceremony on National Day
圣诞礼物 Christmas gift
圣诞卡 Christmas card
新年礼物 New Year's gift
国定假日 national holiday
宗教节日 religious festival
生日蛋糕 birthday cake
生日蜡烛 birthday candle
光棍节 single's day

film 电影

必备 全景影片 panorama [ˌpænəˈrɑːmə] *n.*
西部电影 Western [ˈwestən] *n.*
惊险恐怖片 thriller [ˈθrɪlə(r)] *n.*
音乐片 musical [ˈmjuːzɪkl] *n.*
新闻片 newsreel [ˈnjuːzriːl] *n.*
旅游记录片 travelogue [ˈtrævəlɒg] *n.*
纪录片 documentary [ˌdɒkjʊˈmentrɪ] *n.*
毁灭性的 destructive [dɪˈstrʌktɪv] *adj.*
导演 director [dɪˈrektə(r)] *n.*
电影节 film festival

有教育意义的 instructive [ɪn'strʌktɪv] *adj.*
无声片 silent film
黑白影片 black-and-white film
宽银幕影片 wide screen film
立体影片 3-D movie
动画片 animated cartoon
艺术影片 art film
战争片 war film
历史影片 historical film
教育影片 instructional film
科幻影片 science-fiction movie
灾难片 disaster film
故事片 feature film
动作片 action film
地下电影 underground film
色情电影 porn film / blue film
成人电影 adult movie
外国译制片 dubbed foreign film
重映片 rerun film
特效 special effect
大场景 big scenes
特殊场合 special occasions
戛纳国际电影节 Cannes International Film Festival
威尼斯国际影展 Venice International Movie Festival
柏林国际电影节 Berlin International Film Festival
东京国际电影节 Tokyo International Film Festival
台湾金马电影节 Taipei Golden Horse Film Festival
香港国际电影节 Hong Kong International Film Festival

选 记 普通级的 general ['dʒenrəl] *adj.*

限制级的 restricted [rɪ'strɪktɪd] *adj.*

提名 nomination [ˌnɒmɪ'neɪʃn] *n.*

电影等级 film rating

成人电影 X-rated

辅导级 parental guidance

特别奖 special award

荣誉奖 honorary award

最佳影片奖 best film award

标准银幕 standard screen

宽银幕 wide screen

放映时间 running time

早场 morning show

日场 day show

夜场 evening show

午夜场 late show

电影广告 movie advertisement

friend 朋友

Tips: 适用于 a friend (一个朋友)、a successful person (一个成功的人)、a neighbor (一个邻居)、advantages of your personality (描述你性格中的优势)、a person you would like to talk with (描述你想和他 / 她聊天的人) 和 a person who spoke a different language (描述一个外国人) 。

必 备 聊天 chat [tʃæt] *n.*

误解 misunderstanding [ˌmɪsˌʌndə'stændɪŋ] *n.*

值得信任的 trustworthy ['trʌstwɜːðɪ] *adj.*

善解人意的 considerate [kən'sɪdərət] *adj.*

小区 community [kə'mjuːnətɪ] *n.*

因素 factor ['fæktə(r)] *n.*

承认 recognition [ˌrekəg'nɪʃn] *n.*

机会 opportunity [ˌɒpəˈtjuːnətɪ] *n.*
坚持不懈 perseverance [ˌpɜːsɪˈvɪərəns] *n.*
古董 antique [ænˈtiːk] *n.*
紧急情况 emergency [ɪˈmɜːdʒənsɪ] *n.*
关系 relationship [rɪˈleɪʃnʃɪp] *n.*
预防措施 precaution [prɪˈkɔːʃn] *n.*
好客的 hospitable [hɒˈspɪtəbl] *adj.*
慷慨的 generous [ˈdʒenərəs] *adj.*
幽默的 humorous [ˈhjuːmərəs] *adj.*
聪明的 intelligent [ɪnˈtelɪdʒənt] *adj.*
多才多艺的 versatile [ˈvɜːsətaɪl] *adj.*
外向的 extrovert [ˈekstrəvɜːt] *adj.*
内向的 introvert [ˈɪntrəvɜːt] *adj.*
安静的 quiet [ˈkwaɪət] *adj.*
健谈的 talkative [ˈtɔːkətɪv] *adj.*
野心勃勃的 ambitious [æmˈbɪʃəs] *adj.*
不屈不挠的 persistent [pəˈsɪstəns] *adj.*
获得 attain [əˈteɪn] *v.*
达到 achieve [əˈtʃiːv] *v.*
特征 characteristic [ˌkærəktəˈrɪstɪk] *n.*
代 generation [ˌdʒenəˈreɪʃn] *n.*
乐观的 optimistic [ˌɒptɪˈmɪstɪk] *adj.*
成功的 successful [səkˈsesfl] *adj.*
放弃 surrender [səˈrendə(r)] *v.*
唱卡拉OK sing karaoke
分享快乐和悲伤 share happiness and sadness
陷入麻烦 in trouble
去餐馆 go to restaurants
去钓鱼 go fishing

绝交 break up
共同兴趣 mutual interest
充满活力而且活跃的 energetic and active
慷慨且幽默的 generous and humorous
发送电子邮件或短信 send emails or short messages
庆祝生日 celebrate birthdays
感觉孤独 feel lonely
诉说秘密 tell them secrets
受伤 be hurt
朋友性格变化 change of friends in personality
搬家 move to another place
没有共同之处 do not have anything in common
没有共同兴趣 no same interest
好的听众 good listener
爬山 go to the mountains
朋友圈 circle of friends
感到骄傲 feel proud
享受奢华的生活 enjoy luxurious life
成功的标志 indicators of success
社会地位 social status
大众 the public
天赋和智力 talent and intelligence
满足基本的需要 satisfy the basic demand
房地产 real estate
获得成功 achieve success
友好的气氛 friendly atmosphere
热心的 warm-hearted
不信任感 sense of distrust
对……负责 be responsible for

犯罪率 crime rate
空闲生活 leisure life
攀岩 rock-climbing
随和的 easy-going
个人价值 personal value

furniture 家具

Tips: 适用于 a piece of furniture (一件家具)。

必备 家具 furniture ['fɜːnɪtʃə] *n.*
衣柜 wardrobe ['wɔːdrəʊb] *n.*
书架 bookcase ['bʊkkeɪs] *n.*
屏风 screen [skriːn] *n.*
扶手椅 armchair ['ɑːmtʃeə] *n.*
竹子 bamboo [bæm'buː] *n.*
轻轻摆动 rock [rɒk] *n.*
天然的 natural ['nætʃrəl] *adj.*
材料 material [mə'tɪərɪəl] *n.*
布艺 fabric ['fæbrɪk] *n.*
古董 antique [æn'tiːk] *n.*
红木 rosewood ['rəʊzwʊd] *n.*
皮制的 leather ['leðə(r)] *n.*
木质的 wood [wʊd] *n.*
布 cloth [klɒθ] *n.*
舒适 comfort ['kʌmfət] *n.*
功能 function ['fʌŋkʃn] *n.*
因素 factor ['fæktə(r)] *n.*
尺寸 size [saɪz] *n.*
持久的 durable ['djʊərəbl] *adj.*
继承 inherit [ɪn'herɪt] *v.*
床头柜 bedside table / night table

摇椅 rocking chair
茶几 tea-table
起居室 living room
感觉到摇摆的节奏 feel the rhythm of rocking
环保的 environmental [ɪnˌvaɪərənˈmentl] *adj.*
根据我的要求 according to my requirement
得到完全的放松 get total relaxation
家具商店 furniture shop
做最终的决定 make the final decision
西方国家 western countries
选择家具 choose furniture
引人注意的颜色 striking colors
东方国家 oriental countries
传统风格 traditional styles
有创造性和充满灵感 be creative and full of inspiration
充满想象力 be full of imagination
艺术的感觉 the sense of art
更换家具 change the furniture
实木 solid wood
买家具 buy furniture
明亮的颜色 bright color
有这种感觉 have the feeling
使高兴 cheer up
感觉温暖舒适 feel cozy
家居的材质 material of the furniture
餐桌 dining table
沙发 sofa
和谐的 be in harmony
屋子装饰 room decoration

办公室家具 office furniture
奢侈的 luxurious [lʌg'ʒʊərɪəs] *adj.*
一代一代 from generation to generation
前人的生活方式 lifestyle of predecessors
历史中的根源或痕迹 root or trace in history
最好的见证 best witnesses
历史事件的标志 symbol of historical events
人类社会的进化 evolution of human society

选记 床垫 cushion ['kʊʃn] *n.*
毯子 blanket ['blæŋkɪt] *n.*
枕头 pillow ['pɪləʊ] *n.*
被单 sheet [ʃiːt] *n.*
棉被 quilt [kwɪlt] n
小地毯 rug [rʌg] *n.*
通风机 ventilator ['ventɪleɪtə] *n.*
花瓶 vase [vɑːz] *n.*
餐具 tableware ['teɪblweə] *n.*
茶碟 saucer ['sɔːsə] *n.*
叉 fork [fɔːk] *n.*
茶匙 teaspoon ['tiːspuːn] *n.*
汤匙 tablespoon ['teɪblspuːn] *n.*
筷 chopsticks ['tʃɒpstɪks] *n.*
茶壶 teapot ['tiːpɒt] *n.*
餐巾 napkin ['næpkɪn] *n.*
牙签 toothpick ['tuːθˌpɪk] *n.*
账单 bill [bɪl] *n.*
收据 receipt [rɪ'siːt] *n.*
热水瓶 thermos flask
中央供暖设备 central heating system

落地灯 floor lamp

灯罩 lamp shade

插花 flower arrangement

茶杯 tea cup

汤盆 soup plate

咖啡壶 coffee-pot

桌布 table cloth

game 游戏

必备 激烈的 fierce [fɪəs] *adj.*

需要脑力 require intelligence

身体健康 physical health

使人们更强壮 make people stronger

彼此合作 cooperate with each other

遵照游戏规则 follow rules of games

幼稚并且荒谬的 childish and ridiculous

有他们的游戏时间 have their game time

有很强的竞争 have strong competition

玩玻璃弹球 play marbles

计算机游戏 computer games

留下深深的印记 leave deep traces

引导他们的行为 conduct their behaviors

跳绳 jumping rope

跳房子 play hopscotch

蹦极跳 Bungee jumping

捉人游戏 play tag

玩羊拐 play with dibs

玩过家家 play with doll's house

弹石弹 (弹玻璃球) play marbles

玩积木 play with magic cubes

玩橡皮泥 play with plasticene
抽陀螺 spin top

gift 礼物

必备 香水 perfume ['pɜːfjuːm] *n.*
打火机 lighter ['laɪtə(r)] *n.*
杂志 magazine [ˌmægə'ziːn] *n.*
电器 appliance [ə'plaɪəns] *n.*
领带 tie [taɪ] *n.*
皮带 belt [belt] *n.*
刮胡刀 razor ['reɪzə(r)] *n.*
运动装 sports-wear *n.*
手表 watch [wɒtʃ] *n.*
化妆品 cosmetics [kɒz'metɪk] *n.*
珠宝 jewelry ['dʒuːəlrɪ] *n.*

help 帮助

Tips: 适用于 a person you helped (你帮助过的人) 和 a person who helped you (帮过你的人)。

必备 生存 survive [sə'vaɪv] *v.*
收容所 shelter ['ʃeltə(r)] *n.*
建议 advice [əd'vaɪs] *n.*
乞丐 beggar ['begə(r)] *n.*
帮助穷人 help the poor
政府拨款 government grants
满足基本需要 satisfy basic needs
工作机会 working opportunities
最低收入 minimum income
红十字会 Red Cross
慈善组织 charity organization
接受捐助 receive donations

被分发给有需要的人 be distributed to those in need
娱乐活动 entertainment activities
缺乏信息 lack information
养活他们自己 support themselves
放松并且平静的 relaxed and peaceful
得病 fall sick
财务支持 financial support
捐钱 donate money
自然灾害 natural disaster

historical place 历史古迹

必备 塔，宝塔 pagoda [pə'gəʊdə] *n.*
庙 temple ['templ] *n.*
楼层 storey ['stɔːrɪ] *n.*
到处扔垃圾 litter ['lɪtə(r)] *v.*
保护 preservation [ˌprezə'veɪʃn] *n.*
三角架 tripod ['traɪpɒd] *n.*
有趣的建筑 interesting building
佛像雕塑 Buddha statue
白色大理石 white marble
不同形状 different shape
优雅且高贵的 elegant and stately
民族风格 ethnic style
旅游设施 tourism facilities
历史的见证 witnesses of history
提升旅游业 increase the tourism
当地的经济 local economy
增加收入 increase income
乱涂名字 scribble names
国家财富 national treasure

hobby 爱好

Tips: 适用于任何关于爱好方面的问题或卡片。例如：your hobby (爱好)、your favorite film (最喜爱的电影) 和 your favorite music (最喜爱的音乐)。

必备 唱歌 singing ['sɪŋɪŋ] *n.*

画画 drawing ['drɔːɪŋ] *n.*

消耗 consume [kən'sjuːm] *n.*

破坏 spoil [spɔɪl] *n.*

身体锻炼 physical exercise

拓宽视野 broaden our eyesight

空闲事件 spare time

释放压力 release stress

丰富空闲时光 enrich spare time

holiday 假期

Tips: 适用于 an exciting experience you had (一次有趣的经历) 和 a difficulty thing you did (你做过的一件难事)等。

必备 快乐 happiness ['hæpɪnɪs] *n.*

参与者 participant [pɑː'tɪsɪpənt] *n.*

目的地 destination [ˌdestɪ'neɪʃn] *n.*

旅程 journey ['dʒɜːnɪ] *n.*

海岸线 coastline ['kəʊstlaɪn] *n.*

完美的 perfect ['pɜːfɪkt] *adj.*

毛毛雨 drizzle ['drɪzl] *n.*

坍塌 collapse [kə'læps] *v.*

尖叫 scream [skriːm] *v.*

鸟笼 birdcage ['bɜːdkeɪdʒ] *n.*

雾 fog [fɒg] *n.*

本地人 local people

挑战 challenge ['tʃælɪndʒ] *n.*

保护 protection [prə'tekʃn] *n.*
乐趣 fun [fʌn] *n.*
禁令 ban [bæn] *n.*
设施 facility [fə'sɪlɪtɪ] *n.*
幸存 survival [sə'vaɪvl] *n.*
冒险 adventure [əd'ventʃə(r)] *n.*
潜力 potential [pə'tenʃl] *n.*
效率 efficiency [ɪ'fɪʃnsɪ] *n.*
野心 ambition [æm'bɪʃn] *n.*
激发……兴趣 motivate ['məʊtɪveɪt] *v.*
事故 accident ['æksɪdənt] *n.*
启发 enlighten [ɪn'laɪtn] *v.*
信心 confidence ['kɒnfɪdəns] *n.*
创造力 creativity [ˌkriːeɪ'tɪvətɪ] *n.*
机会 opportunity [ˌɒpə'tjuːnətɪ] *n.*
能力 ability [ə'bɪlətɪ] *n.*
目标 goal [gəʊl] *n.*
达到 achieve [ə'tʃiːv] *v.*
激励 stimulate ['stɪmjʊleɪt] *v.*
专横的 bossy ['bɒsɪ] *adj.*
咨询 consult [kən'sʌlt] *v.*
推荐 recommend [ˌrekə'mend] *v.*
自由 freedom ['friːdəm] *n.*
天真的 naive [naɪ'iːv] *adj.*
成功的 successful [sək'sesfʊl] *adj.*
怀旧的 nostalgic [nɒ'stældʒɪk] *adj.*
成熟的 mature [mə'tjʊə(r)] *adj.*
深刻印象 deep impression
感到疲倦和不情愿 feel tired and reluctant

克服任何困难 overcome difficulty
感到筋疲力尽 feel exhausted
延长假期时间 prolong time of holidays
刺激经济发展 stimulate development of economy
景点 scenic spots
本地经济 local economy
采取措施 take measures to
第三产业 tertiary industry
本地经济的繁荣 prosperity of local economy
造成环境污染 cause environmental pollution
破坏自然景观 spoil natural scenery
访友 visit from others
漫步 wander around
探察城市 explore the city
去划船 go boating
看雕塑和灯笼 see sculptures and lanterns
带来茶叶 bring tea
文化冲击 cultural shock
误解 misunderstanding
感到不舒服 feel uncomfortable
西式 western style
游览这个城市 show around the city
品尝传统食物 taste traditional food
内地人 inland people
轻松地叹气 sigh of relief
危险的冒险活动 dangerous adventure activities
爬山 mountain climbing
极限运动 extreme games
生活的刺激 excitement of life

专业技能 professional skill
喜好疯狂的游戏 enjoy crazy games
去蹦级 go bungee jumping
杀人游戏 killing game
坚持不懈 perseverance [ˌpɜːsɪˈvɪərəns] *n.*
失去信心 lose confidence
分析形势 analyze situation
解决问题 solve the problem
获得经验 gain experience
感到厌烦 feel bored
对成年人的影响 influence on adults
起起落落 ups and downs
复杂的世界 complex world
高期望 have high expectations
引起心理问题 cause psychological problems
作出更大的成就 make greater achievement
安全保障 safety and security
犯罪率 crime rate
平静的世界 peaceful world
积极的想法 positive ideas
做晨练 do morning exercise
环境污染 environmental pollution
平等的工作机会 equal working opportunities
家务的负担 burden of housework
家庭暴力 domestic violence
保护妇女权利 protect rights of women
人们的价值 people's value
大家庭 extended families
小家庭 nuclear families

丁克家庭（双收入没有孩子）DINK families
赢得奖学金 win scholarship
完成一项设计 fulfill a design
献身于 devote to
巨大的成功 great success
被奖励奖学金 be rewarded scholarship
成功的必要条件 necessities of success
努力工作 hard working
感到满足 feel satisfied
最近的成功 recent success
作出决定 make the decision
分析优势和劣势 analyze the advantages and disadvantages
妨碍 interfere with
留下印记 leaves a trace
快乐的童年 happy childhood
健康的生活方式 healthy lifestyle
心理上的能力 mental ability
学习乐器 learn musical instruments

hotel 酒店

Tips: 适用于 a hotel (你住过的酒店)。

必备 桑拿浴 sauna ['sɔːnə] *n.*
家具陈设 furnishing ['fɜːnɪʃɪŋ] *n.*
接待员 receptionist [rɪ'sepʃənɪst] *n.*
箱子 suitcase ['suːtkeɪs] *n.*
大门口 entrance ['entrəns] *n.*
门厅 lobby ['lɒbɪ] *n.*
休息室，起居室 lounge [laʊndʒ] *n.*
走廊 corridor ['kɒrɪdɔː(r)] *n.*
外廊 verandah [və'rændə] *n.*

楼梯 staircase ['steə(r)keɪs] *n.*

电梯 elevator ['elɪveɪtə(r)] *n.*

电梯 lift [lɪft] *n.*

小餐厅 buffet ['bʊfeɪ] *n.*

喷水池 fountain ['faʊntɪn] *n.*

院子 courtyard ['kɔːtjɑːd] *n.*

总统套房 penthouse ['penthaʊs] *n.*

总统套房 presidential suite

套间 suite [swiːt] *n.*

标准间 standard room

浴盆 bathtub ['bɑːθtʌb] *n.*

脸盆 basin ['beɪsn] *n.*

浴衣 bathrobe ['bɑːθrəʊb] *n.*

窗帘 curtain ['kɜːtn] *n.*

百叶窗 shutter ['ʃʌtə(r)] *n.*

百叶窗 blind [blaɪnd] *n.*

五星级饭店 5-star hotel

健身中心 fitness center

商务中心 business center

美容院 beauty salon

康乐中心 health club

会议室 conference room

按摩服务 massage service

出租车服务 taxi service

礼品店 gift shop

室内游泳池 indoor swimming pool

蒸气浴 steam bath

宴会厅 banquet hall

问询处 information desk

旅馆登记簿 hotel register

衣帽间 cloak room

售报处 news-stand

屋顶花园 roof garden

单人房间 single room

双人房间 double room

双床房间 twin-bed room

豪华套间 deluxe suite

窗台 window-sill

梳妆台 dressing-table

衣架 clothes-hanger

健身房 fitness room

弹子房 billiard room

早叫醒 give the morning call

洗衣服 do the laundry

吊床 hammock ['hæmək] *n.*

选 记 盥洗室 washroom ['wɒʃrʊm] *n.*

盥洗室 toilet ['tɔɪlɪt] *n.*

盥洗室 lavatory ['lævətrɪ] *n.*

淋浴 shower bath

淋浴 shower ['ʃaʊə(r)] *n.*

指甲刷 nailbrush ['neɪlbrʌʃ] *n.*

水龙头 faucet ['fɔːsɪt] *n.*

厨房 kitchen ['kɪtʃɪn] *n.*

起居室 living room

起居室 sitting ['sɪtɪŋ] *n.*

客厅 parlour ['pɑːlə(r)] *n.*

客厅 parlor ['pɑːlə(r)] *n.*

工作室 studio ['stjuːdɪəʊ] *n.*

图书室 library ['laɪbrərɪ] *n.*

卧室 bedroom ['bedrʊm] *n.*

厕所 lavatory ['lævətrɪ] *n.*

储藏室 storeroom ['stɔː(r)rʊm] *n.*

地下室 basement ['beɪsmənt] *n.*

阁楼 attic ['ætɪk] *n.*

阁楼 loft [lɒft] *n.*

庭院 courtyard ['kɔːtjɑːd] *n.*

后院 backyard [ˌbæk'jɑːd] *n.*

花园 garden ['gɑːdn] *n.*

草坪 lawn [lɔːn] *n.*

宾馆 hotel [həʊ'tel] *n.*

服务员 attendant [ə'tendənt] *n.*

服务员 hotel boy

水床 water bed

淋浴幕 shower curtain

肥皂缸 soap dish

毛巾架 towel rail

海绵浴擦 bath sponge

背刷 back brush

按摩刷 massage brush

发刷 hair brush

牙刷 tooth brush

牙膏 tooth paste

手纸 toilet paper

管道煤气 pipe-line gas

灭火器 fire extinguisher

前屋 front room

会客室 reception room

餐室 dining room

闲置卧室 spare room

接待处 reception desk

宾馆经理 hotel manager

值班服务员 desk clerk

宾馆接待厅 hotel vestibule

housework 家务活

Tips: 适用于关于家务活的问题。

必备 洗 wash [wɒʃ] *v.*

清洁的 clean [kliːn] *adj.*

刮擦 scrub [skrʌb] *n.*

海绵 sponge [spʌndʒ] *n.*

擦 wipe [waɪp] *v.*

干洗 dry-clean

熨烫 iron ['aɪən] *v.*

抛光 polish ['pəʊlɪʃ] *v.*

整理 tidy ['taɪdɪ] *v.*

housing 住房

Tips: 适用于关于住所的问题。例如：your favorite room / apartment / house (最喜爱的房间 / 公寓 / 房子) 和 a place in your childhood (童年待过的一个地方)。

必备 阳台 balcony ['bælkənɪ] *n.*

卧室 bedroom ['bedruːm] *n.*

浴室 bathroom ['bɑːθruːm] *n.*

书房 study ['stʌdɪ] *n.*

顶楼 attic ['ætɪk] *n.*

地下室 basement ['beɪsmənt] *n.*

大厅 hall [hɔːl] *n.*

门廊 porch [pɔːtʃ] *n.*

游戏室 playroom ['pleɪruːm] *n.*
家具 furniture ['fɜːnɪtʃə(r)] *n.*
地毯 carpet ['kɑːpɪt] *n.*
扶手椅 armchair ['ɑːmtʃə(r)] *n.*
窗帘 drape [dreɪp] *n.*
电冰箱 fridge [frɪdʒ] *n.*
洗涤槽 sink [sɪŋk] *n.*
水龙头 tap [tæp] *n.*
凳子 stool [stuːl] *n.*
炉具 cooker ['kʊkə(r)] *n.*
烤箱 oven ['ʌvn] *n.*
碗柜 cupboard ['kʌbəd] *n.*
水壶 kettle ['ketl] *n.*
锅 saucepan ['sɔːspən] *n.*
抽油烟机 range hood
倒塌，坍塌 collapse [kə'læps] *v.*
遮蔽；收容所 shelter ['ʃeltə(r)] *n.*
竹子 bamboo [bæm'buː] *n.*
屋顶 roof [ruːf] *n.*
斜坡 slope [sləʊp] *n.*
生活方式 lifestyle ['laɪfstaɪl] *n.*
继承 inherit [ɪn'herɪt] *vt.*
节奏 rhythm ['rɪðəm] *n.*
装饰 decoration [ˌdekə'reɪʃn] *n.*
平房 bungalow ['bʌŋgələʊ] *n.*
浴室 bathroom ['bɑːθruːm] *n.*
舒服的 comfortable ['kʌmftəbl] *adj.*
阳光 sunshine ['sʌnʃaɪn] *n.*
无家可归的 homeless ['həʊmlɪs] *adj.*

餐厅 dining room
杂用间 utility room
空房间 spare room
CD 播放机 CD player
高保真音响设备 hi-fi
音箱系统 stereo system
咖啡桌 coffee table
遥控 remote control
食物搅拌机 food mixer
平底煎锅 frying pan
五斗橱 chest of drawers
拆除 tear down
建筑材料 construction material
粘土或干草 clay or hay
夜生活 night life
宽敞的屋子 spacious rooms
吵闹的社区 noisy community
规章制度 rules and regulations
不同的习惯 different habits
起居室 living room
新空气 fresh air
生存空间 living space
大量人口 large population
控制人口 control population
摩天大楼 skyscrapers
容纳更多的人 accommodate more people

选记 电灯 lamp [læmp] *n.*
枕头 pillow ['pɪləʊ] *n.*
衣柜 wardrobe ['wɔːdrəʊb] *n.*

洗澡，沐浴 bath [bɑːθ] *n.*

喷头 shower [ˈʃaʊ(r)] *n.*

毛巾 towel [ˈtaʊəl] *n.*

镜子 mirror [ˈmɪrə(r)] *n.*

洗脸盆 washbasin [ˈwɒʃbeɪsn] *n.*

屋顶 ceiling [ˈsiːlɪŋ] *n.*

暖气 heater [ˈhiːtə] *n.*

电 electricity [ɪˌlekˈtrɪsətɪ] *n.*

闹钟 alarm clock

摇椅 rocking chair

现代设施 modern facility

空调 air-conditioner

language of flowers 花语

Tips: 适用于关于花的问题。

必备 鲜花 flowers [ˈflaʊə(r)z] *n.*

水仙花 narcissus [nɑːˈsɪsəs] *n.*

雏菊 daisy [ˈdeɪzɪ] *n.*

兰花 orchid [ˈɔːkɪd] *n.*

康乃馨 carnation [kɑːˈneɪʃn] *n.*

向日葵 sunflower [ˈsʌnflaʊə(r)] *n.*

蒲公英 dandelion [ˈdændɪlaɪən] *n.*

勿忘我 forget-me-not

满天星 gypsophila [dʒɪpˈsɒfɪlə] *n.*

黄刺玫 yellow rose

睡莲 water lily

开业 open a new business

愉快的气氛 happy atmosphere

舒适浪漫 cozy and romantic

植物园 botanic garden

金凤花 buttercup ['bʌtəkʌp] *n.*
百合 lily ['lɪlɪ] *n.*
郁金香 tulip ['tjuːlɪp] *n.*
紫罗兰 violet ['vaɪələt] *n.*
菊花 chrysanthemum [krɪ'sænθɪməm] *n.*
雪花莲 snowdrop ['snəʊdrɒp] *n.*
丁香 lilac ['laɪlək] *n.*
茉莉 jasmine ['dʒæsmɪn] *n.*
牡丹 peony ['piːənɪ] *n.*
仙人掌 cactus ['kæktəs] *n.*
山茶花 camellia [kə'miːlɪə] *n.*
梅花 plum blossom
桃花 peach blossom
樱桃花 cherry blossom

language 语言

Tips: 适用于关于语言的问题。例如：an activity in an English class (英语课上的一次活动)。

必备 普通话 mandarin ['mændərɪn] *n.*
粤语 Cantonese [ˌkæntə'niːz] *n.*
生动的 vivid ['vɪvɪd] *adj.*
词汇 vocabulary [və'kæbjʊlərɪ] *n.*
交流 communicate [kə'mjuːnɪkeɪt] *v.*
方言 dialect ['daɪəlekt] *n.*
母语 native language
本地方言 local dialect
背单词 memorize words
记忆 memory ['memərɪ] *n.*
英语的重要性 importance of English
讲英文故事 tell English stories

激发兴趣 arouse the interest
对沟通有帮助 useful for communication
掌握这门语言 grasp the language
本族语者 native speakers
英语环境 English speaking environment
必修课程 required course
语感 language intuition
世界和平 world peace

law 法律

必备 法学 Science of Law
法律史 Legal History
宪法学与行政法学 Constitutional Law and Administrative Law
诉讼法学 Science of Procedure Laws
经济法学 Science of Economic Law
国际法学 International Law
军事法学 Science of Military Law
刑法 Criminal Law
行政法 Administrative Law
民法 Civil Law
商法 Commercial Law
自然法 Natural Law
劳工法 Labour Law
财政法 Fiscal Law
军法 Military Law
著作权法 Copyright Law
民事权利，公民权利 civil rights
关税 customs duties
遗产税 death duty / death tax
版税 royalty ['rɔɪəltɪ] *n.*

法案，草案 draft [drɑːft] *n.*
政府议案 government bill
通过议案 pass a bil / carry a bill
颁布法律 enact a law / promulgate a law
法律的实施 law enforcement
生效 come into force
立法 legislation [ˌledʒɪsˈleɪʃn] *n.*
立法者 legislator [ˈledʒɪsleɪtə(r)] *n.*
法制，合法 legality [liːˈgælətɪ] *n.*
法制，合法 lawfulness [ˈlɔːflnɪs] *n.*
合法的，依法的 legal [ˈliːgl] *adj.*
合法的，依法的 lawful [ˈlɔːfl] *adj.*
违法 contravene a law / infringe a law / break a law
超出法律范围的 outlaw [ˈaʊtlɔː] *adj.*
超出法律范围的 outside the law
废止，取消 abolish [əˈbɒlɪʃ] *v.*
豁免，豁免权 immunity [ɪˈmjuːnətɪ] *n.*

leader 领导

必备 视野 vision [ˈvɪʒn] *n.*
实际观点 practical ideas
责任 responsibility [rɪˌspɒnsəˈbɪlətɪ] *n.*
激情 passion [ˈpæʃn] *n.*
幽默 humor [ˈhjuːmə(r)] *n.*
性格强势 strength of character
成熟 maturity [məˈtjuərətɪ] *n.*
耐心 patience [ˈpeɪʃns] *n.*
智慧 wisdom [ˈwɪzdəm] *n.*
常识 common sense
值得信任感 trustworthiness [ˈtrʌstˌwɜːðɪnɪs] *n.*

可靠 reliability [rɪˌlaɪə'bɪlətɪ] *n.*

创造力 creativity [ˌkriːeɪ'tɪvətɪ] *n.*

敏感 sensitivity [ˌsensə'tɪvətɪ] *n.*

商业远见 business foresight

权力 power ['paʊə(r)] *n.*

组织 organization [ˌɔːgənaɪ'zeɪʃn] *n.*

沟通 communication [kəˌmjuːnɪ'keɪʃn] *n.*

乐观 optimism ['ɒptɪmɪzəm] *n.*

管理 management ['mænɪdʒmənt] *n.*

letter 书信

Tips: 适用于 a letter (收到的信)。

必备 电话 telephone calls

传统且保守的 traditional and conservative

联系朋友 contact friends

邮局 post office

邮票和信封 stamps and envelopes

偏僻区域 remote area

情书 love letter

邀请函 invitation letter

辞职信 resignation letter

绝交信 Dear John letter

library 图书馆

Tips: 适用于a library (图书馆)。

必备 标签 tag [tæg] *n.*

续借 renewal [rɪ'njuːəl] *n.*

赔偿 compensation [ˌkɒmpen'seɪʃn] *n.*

书展 book exhibition

极爱读书的人 bookworm ['bʊkwɜːm] *n.*

静电复印机 Xerox ['zɪərɒks] *n.*

城市图书馆 city library
农村图书馆 rural library
省图书馆 provincial library
市图书馆 municipal library
县图书馆 county library
巡回图书馆 circulating library
办公室 administrative office
珍本部 rare books division
书库 stack room
参考阅览室 reference reading room
书名卡 title card
书名目录 catalogue of titles
分类目录 classified catalogue
书名索引 title index
作者索引 author index
分类索引 classified index
联合图书目录 union catalogue
借阅登记 loan registration
借书人 book borrower
借书证 library card
复印室 duplication room
自动还书机 drop box

选记 书签 bookmarker ['bʊkmɑːkə] *n.*
书橱 bookcase ['bʊkkeɪs] *n.*
看书架 bookrack ['bʊkræk] *n.*
平装书 paperback ['peɪpəbæk] *n.*
精装书 hardback ['hɑːdbæk] *n.*
布面书 clothback ['klɒθbæk] *n.*
目录 content ['kɒntent] *n.*

百科全书 encyclopedia [ɪnˌsaɪklə'piːdɪə] *n.*
手稿 manuscript ['mænjʊskrɪpt] *n.*
地图集 atlas ['ætləs] *n.*
小册子 booklet ['bʊklɪt] *n.*
小册子 pamphlet ['pæmflɪt] *n.*
戏剧 drama ['drɑːmə] *n.*
评论 commentary ['kɒməntrɪ] *n.*
社论 editorial [ˌedɪ'tɔːrɪəl] *n.*
选集 anthology [æn'θɒlədʒɪ] *n.*
历书 almanac ['ɔːlmənæk] *n.*
录像带 videotape ['vɪdɪəʊteɪp] *n.*
报夹 newspaper binder
杂志夹 magazine binder
期刊架 periodical rack
珍本 rare book
孤本 the only existing copy
秘本 treasured copy of a rare book
赠阅本 presentation copy
简写本 simplified edition
改写本 adapted edition
缩印本 compact edition
豪华精装本 deluxe edition
新版 new edition
原版 original edition
初版 first edition
试用版 trial edition
修订版 revised edition
袖珍版 pocket edition
普及版 popular edition

盗印版 pirated edition
封面 front cover
有声读物 talking book
预约的书 reserved book
有插图的书 illustrated book
推荐的书 recommended book
新闻评论 news comment
文艺评论 literary criticism
全集 complete works
参考书籍 reference books
科技书籍 scientific and technical books
医学书籍 medical books
农业书籍 agricultural books
宗教书籍 religious books

magazine and newspaper 期刊杂志

Tips: 适用 favorite book (最喜爱的书)、 favorite magazine or newspaper (最喜爱的报纸或杂志)、 a book you want to write (你想写的一本书) 和 a book you read when you were a child (小时候读过的一本书) 等。

必备 报刊 press [pres] *n.*
画报 pictorial [pɪk'tɔːrɪəl] *n.*
画报 picture magazine
增刊 supplement ['sʌplɪmənt] *n.*
年刊 annual ['ænjʊəl] *n.*
年鉴 almanac ['ɔːlmənæk] *n.*
全国性报刊 national press
官方报纸 official newspaper
政府机关报 government organ
政党机关报 party organ

定期刊物 periodical publication
教育杂志 educational journal
妇女杂志 ladies' magazine
时装杂志 fashion magazine
理论杂志 theoretical magazine
军事杂志 military magazine
新闻杂志 news magazine
双周刊 biweekly magazine
月刊 monthly magazine
双月刊 bimonthly magazine
季刊 quarterly magazine
书店 bookshop ['bʊkʃɒp] *n.*
书店 bookseller ['bʊkselə(r)] *n.*
报刊亭 newsagent ['nju:zˌeɪdʒənt] *n.*
报刊亭 newsstand ['nju:zstænd] *n.*
章节 section ['sekʃn] *n.*
运动 sports [spɔ:ts] *n.*
科学 science ['saɪəns] *n.*
场所 forum ['fɔ:rəm] *n.*
每周的 weekly ['wi:klɪ] *adj.*
每月的 monthly ['mʌnθlɪ] *adj.*
化妆品 cosmetics [kɒz'metɪks] *n.*
衣着 dressing ['dresɪŋ] *n.*
报摊 newsstand ['nju:zstænd] *n.*
不可替代的 irreplaceable [ˌɪrɪ'pleɪsəbl] *adj.*
广告 advertisement [əd'vɜ:tɪsmənt] *n.*
媒体 media ['mi:dɪə] *n.*
外观 appearance [ə'pɪərəns] *n.*
高级的 senior ['si:nɪə(r)] *adj.*

包含 contain [kən'teɪn] *v.*

英语杂志 English magazine

商业信函 business letter

每日杂志 daily magazines

时事 current affairs

专家意见 experts' comment

热门事件 hot issues

强调话题 emphasize topics

每日新闻 daily news

相关信息 related information

全面的理解 comprehensive understanding

丰富每天的生活 enrich daily life

特定专栏 specific columns

优秀的文章 excellent articles

选记 标题 headline ['hedlaɪn] *n.*

封面 cover ['kʌvə(r)] *n.*

前言 foreword ['fɔːwɜːd] *n.*

特写 feature ['fiːtʃə(r)] *n.*

专访 interview ['ɪntəvjuː] *n.*

剧照 still [stɪl] *n.*

人事要闻 personals ['pɜːsnəlz] *n.*

报告文学 reportage [rɪ'pɔːtɪdʒ] *n.*

头版 front page

第二版 second page

增页 supplementary sheet

天气预报 weather forecast

封面女郎 cover girl

封二 inside front

创刊 start publication

创刊号 first issue
封面故事 cover story
特约稿 the special
独家采访 exclusive interview
通讯 news report
报刊评论 press commentary
书评 book review
剧评 play notice
报刊文摘 press digest
连环漫画 strip cartoon
连载故事 running story

media 媒体

必备 新闻业 journalism ['dʒɜːnəlɪzəm] *n.*
新闻工作者 journalist ['dʒɜːnəlɪst] *n.*
报社从业人员 newspaperman ['njuːzpeɪpəmæn] *n.*
报社业主 publisher ['pʌblɪʃə] *n.*
新闻编辑室 newsroom ['njuːzrʊm] *n.*
专栏编辑 columnist ['kɒləmnɪst] *n.*
通俗小报 tabloid ['tæblɔɪd] *n.*
双周刊 biweekly [ˌbaɪ'wiːklɪ] *n.*
半月刊 semimonthly ['semɪ'mʌnθlɪ] *n.*
月刊 monthly ['mʌnθlɪ] *n.*
双月刊 bimonthly [ˌbaɪ'mʌnθlɪ] *n.*
季刊 quarterly ['kwɔːtəlɪ] *n.*
定期刊物 periodical [ˌpɪərɪ'ɒdɪkl] *n.*
报刊杂志社 newspaper and magazine office
报界 the press / journalistic circles
新闻界 the news trade
报业协会 press association

报社 newspaper office
通讯社 news agency / press agency
报业巨头 press baron
新闻评论员 news analyst
大众性报纸 popular paper
年刊 annual magazine
学术期刊 academic journal
合刊 combined issue
公开出版物 public prints
内部出版物 restricted publication
非法出版物 underground publication
过期出版物 back number

money 金钱

Tips: 适用于 what you would do if you had money (有钱如何花)。

必备 时髦的 fashionable ['fæʃnəbl] *adj.*
课税 taxation [tæk'seɪʃn] *n.*
学费 tuition [tju:'ɪʃn] *n.*
富裕的 wealthy ['welθɪ] *adj.*
节日 festival ['festəvl] *n.*
成就 achievement [ə'tʃi:vmənt] *n.*
快艇 yacht [jɒt] *n.*
节俭的 frugal ['fru:gl] *adj.*
奢侈品 luxuries ['lʌkʃərɪz] *n.*
愉快 pleasure ['pleʒə(r)] *n.*
购买 purchase ['pɜ:tʃəs] *v.*
收入 income ['ɪŋkʌm] *n.*
利润 profit ['prɒfɪt] *n.*
教育水平 educational level
蓝领工人 blue-collar workers

计算机编程人员 computer programmer
政府官员 government official
违背法律 violate the laws
钱的来源 source of money
医疗保健 medical care
零用钱 pocket money
额外的钱 extra money
物质东西 material things
社会地位 social status
价值的象征 symbol of value
奢侈的东西 luxurious things
日用品 daily necessities
网上购物 online shopping
财富管理 money management
财务目标 financial goals
省一些钱 set aside some money
携带现金 carry cash
信用卡 credit card
钱的总数 sum of money
安全感 sense of security

museum 博物馆

Tips: 适用于关于博物馆的问题。例如：a museum (博物馆) 和 an exhibition (展览会)。

必备 娱乐 relaxation [ˌriːlækˈseɪʃn] *n.*
组织 organization [ˌɔːɡənaɪˈzeɪʃn] *n.*
进化 evolution [ˌiːvəˈluːʃn] *n.*
用具 utensils [juːˈtensl] *n.*
大英博物馆 British Museum
现代美术博物馆 Museum of Modern Art

故宫博物馆 Palace Museum
自然博物馆 natural museum
军事博物馆 military museum
蜡像馆 wax figure museum
罗浮宫 Louvre Museum
科学博物馆 science museum
公共博物馆 public museum
私人博物馆 private museum
汽车博物馆 car museum
历史博物馆 history museum
艺术博物馆 art museum
新式并且现代的 fresh and modern
原创杰作 original masterpieces
时区 time zone
有成就感 have sense of achievement
有更多的发明创造 have greater inventions or creations
参观展览会 visit exhibitions
拓宽视野 widen their horizon
有深刻的理解 have a vivid understanding
展现创造力和朴素 show the creativity and simplicity
鉴赏作品 appreciate their works
举行更多的活动 hold more activities
毛绒玩具 stuffed animal
激发人们的好奇心 arouse people's curiosity
高科技的运用 application of high technology
背景音乐 background music
保持合适的温度 keep the temperature appropriate
保存有价值的记忆 keep valuable memories
展览会的多样性 variety of exhibitions

迎合需要 cater to the needs
没有兴趣 have no interest
获取过去的信息 gain information about the past
深刻了解文化和文学 insight into culture and literature
收到政府资金 receive fund from the government
邀请专家来讲座 invite experts to give lectures
举行竞赛 hold some competitions
给予奖励 get a prize
做展览 do exhibitions
馆长 director [dɪ'rektə(r)] *n.*
收藏家 collector [kə'lektə(r)] *n.*
鉴赏家 appreciator [ə'pri:ʃɪeɪtə] *n.*
参观者 visitor ['vɪzɪtə(r)] *n.*
参观证 admission ticket
导游 tour guide

music 音乐

必备 音乐家 musician [mjʊ'zɪʃn] *n.*
指挥棒 baton ['bætɒn] *n.*
乐队 band [bænd] *n.*
管弦乐队 orchestra ['ɔ:kɪstrə] *n.*
音乐厅 concert hall
西洋乐器 western instrument
乐队指挥 orchestra conductor
合唱队指挥 chorus master
铜管乐队 brass band
管乐队 wind band
弦乐队 string band / string orchestra
交响乐队 symphony orchestra
军乐队 military band

民乐队 folk orchestra
轻音乐队 light music band
流行乐队 pop group
乐队领队 band leader
专业乐队 professional band
业余乐队 amateur band

name 名字

Tips: 适用于所有关于名字的问题。

必 备 姓氏 surname ['sɜːneɪm] *n.*
姓氏 family name / last name
(姓名中的) 名字 given name / first name

选 记 运气 luck [lʌk] *n.*
迷信的 superstitious [ˌsuːpə'stɪʃəs] *adj.*
好运气 good fortune
家谱 family tree
算命者，看相者 fortune-teller

noise 噪声

必 备 妨碍，打扰 disturb [dɪ'stɜːb] *v.*
听到汽车喇叭 hear the horns
建筑工地 construction site
装修房屋 decorate home
全神贯注地工作 concentrate on one's work
制定规章制度 make rules and regulations
森林里溪流的声音 sound of creek in the forest
空调发出来的噪声 noise of air-conditioners
使……发疯 drive someone crazy

选 记 垃圾 rubbish ['rʌbɪʃ] *n.*
垃圾 garbage ['gɑːbɪdʒ] *n.*
垃圾 waste [weɪst] *n.*

垃圾 trash [træʃ] *n.*
人口过密 overpopulation [ˌəʊvəpɒpjʊˈleɪʃn] *n.*
灭绝 extinction [ɪkˈstɪŋkʃn] *n.*
生态系统 ecosystem [ˈiːkəʊsɪstəm] *n.*
河流污染 stream pollution
河道污染 river pollution
土壤污染 soil pollution
烟污染 smoke pollution
水短缺 shortage of water
生活用水 domestic water
酸雨 acid rain
耗尽资源 exhaust the resources
过度开采 over-exploitation
过度捕杀 excessive hunting
捕捞过度 excessive amount of fishing
毁灭性后果 destructive consequences
全球变暖 global warming
能源枯竭 energy depletion
生态危机 ecological crisis
空气质量危机 air-quality crisis
变化无常的天气 changeable weather
温室效应 greenhouse effect
防污染 anti-pollution
污染控制 pollution control
环境卫生 environmental sanitation

old people 老人

Tips: 适用于 an old person (一个老人)。

必备 保守的 conservative [kənˈsɜːvətɪv] *adj.*
内敛的 reserved [rɪˈzɜːvd] *adj.*

留下生活的印记 leave a trace in life
年长的人 the elders
基本生活必需品 basic daily necessities
免费住宿 free accommodation
政府救济 government relief
拥有自由 have freedom
福利和健康 welfare and health
得到养老金 get their pension
显示权威 show their authority
引起冲突 cause conflicts
不愿接受新思想 reluctant to accept new ideas
阻碍发展 hinder their development
重要事件的组织者 organizers of some important events
精神偶像 spiritual idol
启发我们 enlighten us
耐心和忍耐力 patience and endurance

park 公园

Tips: 适用于关于花园、公园的问题。例如：your favorite park / garden (最喜爱的花园) 和 your holiday (一次假期)。

必备 纳税人 taxpayer ['tækspeɪə(r)] *n.*
宝物，珍宝 treasure ['treʒə(r)] *n.*
昆虫 insect ['ɪnsekt] *n.*
国家公园 national park
游乐园 amusement park
著名的公园 famous park
去划船 go boating
享用美食 enjoy the delicacy
奇怪的现象 weird phenomenon
传统的国家 traditional country

合适的配偶 suitable spouse
教育背景 education background
放松和振奋 relaxed and refreshed
来消遣 have relaxation
每个街区都有公园 a park in every district
公共花园 public gardens
专业的园丁 professional gardeners
做些园艺工作 do some gardening
私人花园 private gardens
清理花园 clean the garden
呼吸新鲜空气 breathe fresh air
玩得开心 have fun
晨练 do morning exercises
玩游戏 play games
有更好情绪 have a better mood
公共设施 public facilities
保护稀有动物 protect rare animals
忍受强烈的阳光 endure the strong sunshine
获得乐趣 get pleasure
看见植物和花儿 see plants and flowers
社会地位的象征 symbol of social status
享受平静的土地 enjoy a peaceful land
独一无二的花园 unique garden

people who are studying 学生

Tips: 在口语考试第一部分，有时会问你的身份。此外还有一些与学习相关的问题会用到下述词汇，例如：your school (你的学校)、your favorite subject (你最喜爱的课程)、a training class (培训课)和 a course you took (你参加过的课程)等。

学校

必备

大学 university [ˌjuːnɪˈvɜːsətɪ] *n.*
学院学校 colleague [ˈkɒlɪdʒ] *n.*
研究所，学院 institute [ˈɪnstɪtjuːt] *n.*
幼儿园 kindergarten [ˈkɪndəɡɑːtn] *n.*
系 faculty [ˈfæklτɪ] *n.*
年级 grade [ɡreɪd] *n.*
系 department [dɪˈpɑːtmənt] *n.*
测验 quiz [kwɪz] *n.*
学费 tuition [tjuˈɪʃn] *n.*
助学金 stipend [ˈstaɪpend] *n.*
奖学金 scholarship [ˈskɒləʃɪp] *n.*
学分 credit [ˈkredɪt] *n.*
注册 register [ˈredʒɪstə(r)] *n.*
教科书 textbook [ˈtekstbʊk] *n.*
教学大纲 syllabus [ˈsɪləbəs] *n.*
视听教材 audiovisuals [ˌɔːdɪəʊˈvɪʒʊəlz] *n.*
图书馆 library [ˈlaɪbrərɪ] *n.*
大礼堂 auditorium [ˌɔːdɪˈtɔːrɪəm] *n.*
操场 playground [ˈpleɪɡraʊnd] *n.*
宿舍 dormitory [ˈdɔːmɪtrɪ] *n.*
医务室 infirmary [ɪnˈfɜːmərɪ] *n.*
学期 term [tɜːm(r)] *n.*
学期 semester [sɪˈmestə] *n.*
住宿 accommodation [əˌkɒməˈdeɪʃn] *n.*
高考 matriculation [məˌtrɪkjʊˈleɪʃn] *n.*
专业的 professional [prəˈfeʃənl] *adj.*
学季 quarter [ˈkwɔːtə(r)] *n.*
创造力 creativity [ˌkriːeɪˈtɪvətɪ] *n.*

风雨操场 all-weather playground

健身房 gymnasium [dʒɪm'neɪzɪəm] *n.*

高中 high school / senior school

中学 middle school

中学 secondary school (英式)

小学 primary school / elementary school

托儿所 nursery school

混合性别的学校 mixed-sex school

单一性别的学校 single-sex school

私立学校 private school

公寓 hall of residence

结业 complete a course

成绩单 school report

学历 educational background

学位 academic degree

教材 teaching material

教具 teaching aid

视听教具 audio-visual aids

语言实验室 language laboratory

阅览室 reading room

游泳池 swimming pool

寒假 winter vacation

暑假 summer vacation

学年 academic year

高级设施 advanced facilities

课外活动 extracurricular activities

学生

一年级大学生 freshman ['freʃmən] *n.*

二年级大学生 sophomore ['sɒfəmɔː(r)] *n.*

三年级大学生 junior ['dʒuːnjə(r)] *n.*
四年级大学生 senior ['sɪːnɪə(r)] *n.*
本科生 undergraduate [ˌʌndə'grædʒuət] *n.*
研究生 postgraduate [ˌpəust'grædʒuət] *n.*
博士生 candidate for doctor's degree
留学生 overseas student

学位

博士后 postdoctoral [ˌpəust'dɒktərəl] *n.*
学士学位 bachelor's degree
文学士 Bachelor of Arts
理学士 Bachelor of Science
硕士学位 master's degree
博士学位 doctor's degree
博士 Doctor of Philosophy
名誉学位 honorary degree

教职工

授课教师 lecturer ['lektʃərə(r)] *n.*
教授 professor [prə'fesə(r)] *n.*
客座教授 visiting professor / guest professor
副教授 associate professor
助教 assistant professor
新生导师 adviser [əd'vaɪzə] *n.*
辅导员 tutor ['tjuːtə(r)] *n.*
大学校长 president ['prezɪdənt] *n.*
访问学者 visiting scholar
教务长 dean of studies
班主任 class supervisor
兼职教师 part-time teacher
稳定的 stable ['steɪbl] *adj.*

有资格 be qualified

有耐心和责任心 have patience and responsibility

讲解知识 explain the knowledge

上课迟到 late for classes

很多空闲时间 a lot of free time

享有不同的嗜好 enjoy different hobbies

师范学院 teacher's college

师范大学 normal university

教师证书或执照 teacher's certificate or license

获取知识 acquire knowledge

受尊敬的工作 respectable job

选 记

音乐学院 conservatory[kən'sɜːvətrɪ] *n.*

毕业生 graduate['grædʒʊət] *n.*

退学学生 dropout['drɒpaʊt] *n.*

男校友 alumnus[ə'lʌmnəs] *n.*

女校友 alumna[ə'lʌmnə] *n.*

课间 break[breɪk] *n.*

作弊 cheat[tʃiːt] *n.*

大专 junior college

研究生院 graduate school

附小 attached primary school

附中 attached secondary school

实验学校 experimental school

职业学校 vocational school

成人学校 adult school

公立学校 public school

艺术学校 art school

师范学校 normal school

全日制学校 full-time school

业余学校 part-time school
函授学校 correspondence school
夜校 evening school / night school
寄宿学校 boarding school
文学院 college of liberal arts
人文学院 college of humanities
商学院 business school
医学院 medical college
幼儿教育 infant education
学前教育 preschool education
初等教育 elementary education
中等教育 secondary education
高等教育 higher education
继续教育 further education
成人教育 adult education
义务教育 compulsory education
大学服装 academic dress
毕业典礼 graduation ceremony
毕业证书 graduation certificate
学期论文 term paper
优秀生 honours student
高材生 top student
应考 take an examination
逃学 play truant
跳级 skip a grade
备课 prepare lessons
打铃 ring the bell
下课 dismiss the class
出卷 make out an examination

试卷 test paper
笔试 written examination
开卷考试 open-book examination
能力测试 aptitude test
考场 examination room
校历 academic calendar
校报 campus newspaper
校刊 college journal
校规 school regulations
校徽 school badge
鼓舞人心的 inspiring [ɪn'spaɪərɪŋ] *adj.*
引人入胜的 intriguing [ɪn'triːgɪŋ] *adj.*
启发 inspire [ɪn'spaɪə(r)] *v.*
有资格的 qualified ['kwɒlɪfaɪd] *adj.*
主课 main course
副课 minor course
选修课 elective course / optional course
必修课 required course / compulsory course
重修课 makeup course
学分课程 credit course
铭记 remain in one's memory
掌握新技能 grasp new skills
提高能力 improve ability
教师的素质 qualities of teachers
有用的信息 useful information
探求答案 explore answers
获得知识 attain knowledge
公众兴趣 general interests
高分 high score

激发兴趣 arouse interests
给建议 give advice
面对面指导 face to face guidance
代数 algebra ['ældʒɪbrə] *n.*
算术 arithmetic [ə'rɪθmətɪk] *n.*
几何 geometry [dʒɪ'ɒmətrɪ] *n.*
历史 history ['hɪstərɪ] *n.*
地理 geography [dʒi'ɒgrəfɪ] *n.*
物理 physics ['fɪzɪks] *n.*
音乐 music ['mjuːzɪk] *n.*
化学 chemistry ['kemɪstrɪ] *n.*
政治 politics ['pɒlɪtɪks] *n.*
图画 drawing ['drɔːɪŋ] *n.*
生物 biology [baɪ'ɒlədʒɪ] *n.*
写字 calligraphy [kə'lɪgrəfɪ] *n.*
生理卫生 physiology [ˌfɪzɪ'ɒlədʒɪ] *n.*
法律学 law [lɔː] *n.*
人类学 anthropology [ˌænθrə'pɒlədʒɪ] *n.*
心理学 psychology [saɪ'kɒlədʒɪ] *n.*
考古学 archaeology [ˌɑːkɪ'ɒlədʒɪ] *n.*
语言学 linguistics [lɪŋ'gwɪstɪks] *n.*
经济学 economics [ˌiːkə'nɒmɪks] *n.*
会计学 accounting [ə'kaʊntɪŋ] *n.*
财务学 finance ['faɪnæns] *n.*
修辞学 rhetoric ['retərɪk] *n.*
统计学 statistics [stə'tɪstɪks] *n.*
社会学 sociology [ˌsəʊsɪ'ɒlədʒɪ] *n.*
教育学 pedagogy ['pedəgɒdʒɪ] *n.*
哲学 philosophy [fɪ'lɒsəfɪ] *n.*

逻辑学 logic ['lɒdʒɪk] *n.*
伦理学 ethics ['eθɪks] *n.*
档案学 archives ['ɑːkaɪvz] *n.*
美学 aesthetics [iːs'θetɪks] *n.*
新闻学 journalism ['dʒɜːnəlɪzəm] *n.*
天文 astronomy [ə'strɒnəmɪ] *n.*
生化学 biochemistry [ˌbaɪəʊ'kemɪstrɪ] *n.*
动物学 zoology [zəʊ'ɒlədʒɪ] *n.*
植物学 botany ['bɒtənɪ] *n.*
力学 mechanics [mɪ'kænɪks] *n.*
矿物学 mineralogy [ˌmɪnə'rælədʒɪ] *n.*
森林学 forestry ['fɒrɪstrɪ] *n.*
电子学 electronics [ˌɪlek'trɒnɪks] *n.*
电学 electricity [ɪˌlek'trɪsətɪ] *n.*
遗传学 genetics [dʒɪ'netɪks] *n.*
生态学 ecology [ɪ'kɒlədʒɪ] *n.*
生理学 physiology [ˌfɪzɪ'ɒlədʒɪ] *n.*
解剖学 anatomy [ə'nætəmɪ] *n.*
免疫学 immunology [ˌɪmjʊ'nɒlədʒɪ] *n.*
外科学 surgery ['sɜːdʒərɪ] *n.*
工艺学 technology [tek'nɒlədʒɪ] *n.*
机械学 mechanics [mɪ'kænɪks] *n.*
建筑学 architecture ['ɑːkɪtektʃə(r)] *n.*
自然 nature study
体育 physical education
美术 fine arts
常识 general knowledge
军训课 military training
文科 liberal arts

世界史 world history
文学批评 literary criticism
企业管理 business administration
国际金融 international finance
政治学 political science
自然辩证法 philosophy of science
形式逻辑学 formal logic
公共关系学 public relations
大众传播学 mass communication
环境与资源生物学 environment and resources biology
计算机科学 computer science

people who are working 工作人群

Tips: 适用于关于职业的问题。例如：a job you want to do (你想从事的一份工作)。

职业类型

画家 painter ['peɪntə(r)] *n.*
牙医 dentist ['dentɪst] *n.*
外科医生 surgeon ['sɜːdʒən] *n.*
内科医生 physician [fɪ'zɪʃn] *n.*
护士 nurse [nɜːs] *n.*
记者 journalist ['dʒɜːnəlɪst] *n.*
工程师 engineer [ˌendʒɪ'nɪə(r)] *n.*
程序员 programmer ['prəʊgræmə] n.
建筑师 architect ['ɑːkɪtekt] *n.*
设计师 designer [dɪ'zaɪnə(r)] *n.*
美发师 hairdresser ['heədresə(r)] *n.*
理发师 barber ['bɑːbə(r)] *n.*
裁缝 tailor ['teɪlə(r)] *n.*
模特 model ['mɒdl] *n.*

摄影师 photographer [fə'tɒgrəfə(r)] *n.*
艺术家 artist ['ɑːtɪst] *n.*
职员 clerk [klɑːk] *n.*
建筑工人 construction worker
警察 police officer
计算机操作员 computer operator

选记

机修工 mechanic [mɪ'kænɪk] *n.*
电工 electrician [ɪˌlek'trɪʃn] *n.*
管子工 plumber ['plʌmə(r)] *n.*
消防员 firefighter ['faɪəfaɪtə] *n.*
渔夫 fisherman ['fɪʃəmən] *n.*
花商 florist ['flɒrɪst] *n.*
杂货商 grocer ['grəʊsə(r)] *n.*
屠夫 butcher ['bʊtʃə(r)] *n.*
面包师 baker ['beɪkə] *n.*
厨师 chef [ʃef] *n.*
服务员 waiter ['weɪtə] *n.*
女服务员 waitress ['weɪtrɪs] *n.*
科学家 scientist ['saɪəntɪst] *n.*
兽医 vet [vet] *n.*
药剂师 pharmacist ['fɑːməsɪst] *n.*
新闻播音员 newscaster ['njuːzˌkɑːstə(r)] *n.*
银行出纳员 teller ['telə(r)] *n.*
售货员，推销员 salesperson ['seɪlzpəːsn] *n.*

有关工作

毕业证书 diploma [dɪ'pləʊmə] *n.*
证书 certificate [sə'tɪfɪkət] *n.*
学位 degree [dɪ'griː] *n.*
谈判 negotiate [nɪ'gəʊʃɪeɪt] *v.*

团队协作 teamwork ['tiːmwɜːk] *n.*
经验 experience [ɪk'spɪərɪəns] *n.*
歧视 discrimination [dɪˌskrɪmɪ'neɪʃn] *n.*
坚持不懈 persistence [pə'sɪstəns] *n.*
自由职业者 freelancer ['friːlɑːnsə] *n.*
野心 ambition [æm'bɪʃn] *n.*
职责 responsibility [rɪˌspɒnsə'bɪlətɪ] *n.*
事业 career [kə'rɪə(r)] *n.*
传统的 traditional [trə'dɪʃənl] *adj.*
面试 interview ['ɪntəvjuː] *n.*
表现 performance [pə'fɔːməns] *n.*
商业合作 business cooperation
性别歧视 sex discrimination
优缺点 strength and weakness
各行各业 all walks of life
出差 go on business trips
享受闲暇时光 enjoy leisure time
感觉放松 feel relaxed / have relaxation
加班 work overtime
筋疲力尽 feel exhausted
计算机技能 computer skills
个人技能 personal skills
报纸广告 newspaper advertisement
找工作 job hunting
人才市场 talent market
固定工作时间 fixed working hours

选记
启发的 enlightening [ɪn'laɪtnɪŋ] *adj.*
决定 decision [dɪ'sɪʒn] *n.*
福利 welfare ['welfeə(r)] *n.*

保险 insurance [ɪn'ʃɔːrəns] *n.*
时间表 timetable ['taɪmteɪbl] *n.*
激烈的 fierce [fɪəs] *adj.*
有压力的 stressful [stresfl] *adj.*
能量 energy ['enədʒɪ] *n.*
激发 motivate ['məʊtɪveɪt] *v.*
合作 cooperation [kəʊˌɒpə'reɪʃn] *n.*
合伙人 partner ['pɑːtnə(r)] *n.*
要求 requirement [rɪ'kwaɪə(r)mənt] *n.*
效率 efficiency [ɪ'fɪʃnsɪ] *n.*
环境 environment [ɪn'vaɪərənmənt] *n.*
个人的 individual [ˌɪndɪ'vɪdʒʊəl] *adj.*
生产力 productivity [ˌprɒdʌk'tɪvətɪ] *n.*
士气 morale [mə'rɑːl] *n.*
程序 process ['prəʊses] *n.*
收益 profit ['prɒfɪt] *n.*
压力 pressure ['preʃə(r)] *n.*
规划 planning [plænɪŋ] *n.*
管理 management ['mænɪdʒmənt] *n.*
市场营销 marketing ['mɑːkɪtɪŋ] *n.*
会计 accounting [ə'kaʊntɪŋ] *n.*
养老保险系统 pension system
住房公积金 legal reserves of housing acquisition
医疗照顾 medical care
闲暇时间 leisure time
工作量 work load
解除压力 relieve pressure
工作联系 connections of work
基本构造 basic structures

美容沙龙 beauty saloons
咖啡店 coffee shop
小餐厅 lounge
解决问题 tackle problems
沟通策略 communication strategies
商法 business law
经济合作 economic co-operation
综合能力 comprehensive abilities
对挑战的反应 response to challenges

photograph 照片

Tips: 适用于关于摄影的问题。例如：your favorite photo (最喜爱的照片)。

必备 人物像 portrait ['pɔːtrɪt] *n.*
半身像 bust [bʌst] *n.*
风景照 scenic ['siːnɪk] *n.*
给……拍照 photograph ['fəʊtəgrɑːf] *v.*
摄影师 photographer ['fəʊtəgrɑːfə] *n.*
业余爱好者 amateur ['æmətə(r)] *n.*
纪念 commemoration [kə,memə'reɪʃn] *n.*
便携的 portable ['pɔːtəbl] *adj.*
近照 recent picture
侧面像 profile photo
全身像 full-length portrait
全家福 family photo
留下最快乐的瞬间 keep happiest moment
摄影俱乐部 photographic club
鉴赏不同的照片 appreciate different photos
拍照片 take pictures
用不同的镜片 use different lenses

冲洗底片 develop films
保留重要的瞬间 keep the important moment
留有甜蜜的回忆 keep the sweet memories
保留珍贵的瞬间 retain precious moments
数码照片 digital photos
游乐场 amusement park
分享经历 share their experience
用数码相机 use digital cameras
上传照片 upload the photos
打印出照片 print the photos out
专业摄影师 professional photographer
名胜 places of interest
古建筑 ancient buildings
自然美 natural beauty
满足我们的需要 satisfy our demand
自动相机 automatic cameras
整体结构 whole structure
用闪光灯 use flashlight
引起人们的注意 attract people's attention
婚礼仪式 wedding ceremony
有吸引力的照片 attractive pictures
吸引人们的注意 draw people's attention

选记

摄影 photography [fə'tɒgrəfɪ] *n.*
镜头 lens [lenz] *n.*
闪光灯 flasher ['flæʃə] *n.*
照相器材 photo supplies
广角镜 wide-angle lens
可变焦距镜头 zoom lens
观景镜 view finder
电池盒 battery container

计数器 film counter

快门按钮 shutter button

relaxation 放松

Tips: 适用于 your favorite relaxation (最喜爱的放松方式)。

必备 成就 accomplishment [ə'kʌmplɪʃmənt] *n.*

胜利 triumph ['traɪʌmf] *n. & v.*

沮丧 frustration [frʌ'streɪʃn] *n.*

压力 stress [stres] *n. & v.*

焦虑 anxiety [æŋ'zaɪətɪ] *n.*

松弛 unwind [ˌʌn'waɪnd] *v.*

冥想 meditation [ˌmedɪ'teɪʃn] *n.*

身体上的 physical ['fɪzɪkl] *adj.*

失眠 insomnia [ɪn'sɒmnɪə] *n.*

胃 stomach ['stʌmək] *n.*

对比 compare [kəm'peə(r)] *v. & n.*

团结 solidarity [ˌsɒlɪ'dærətɪ] *n.*

关注 concern [kən'sɜːn] *v. & n.*

庆祝胜利 celebrate success

提高自尊心 boost self-esteem

每天的消遣 daily relaxation

振奋 be refreshed

心理健康 mental health

购物 go shopping

人际关系 interpersonal relationship

没胃口 lose appetite

压力的起因 cause of stress

restaurant 餐馆

Tips: 适用于关于食物的问题。例如: special meal (特别的一顿饭) 和 favorite restaurant (最喜欢的餐厅)。

必备 咖啡厅 café['kæfeɪ] *n.*
自助餐厅 cafeteria [ˌkæfəˈtɪərɪə] *n.*
食堂 canteen [kænˈtiːn] *n.*
食堂 refectory [rɪˈfektrɪ] *n.*
酒吧 bar [bɑː(r)] *n.*
沙龙 saloon [səˈluːn] *n.*
宴会 feast [fiːst] *n.*
宴会 banquet [ˈbæŋkwɪt] *n.*
自助餐 buffet [ˈbʊfeɪ] *n.*
野餐 picnic [ˈpɪknɪk] *n.*
配方 recipe [ˈresəpɪ] *n.*
旋转餐厅 revolving restaurant
四川饭馆 Sichuan restaurant
小吃吧 snack bar
敏感的胃 sensitive stomach
常客 regular customer
舒适的氛围 cozy atmosphere
感到放松 feel at ease
记住味道 remember taste
中式烹饪 Chinese cuisine
生活节奏 pace of life
食物处理 food processing
传统生产 traditional production
副作用 side effects
营养流失 nutrition loss
聚会 have a get-together
交换信息 exchange information
有更多的选择 have more choices
辣的食物 spicy food

重口味 strong flavor
咸的食物 salty food
预定坐位 reserve seats
提供食物 serve food
装修 decoration [ˌdekəˈreɪʃn] *n.*
优惠券 coupon [ˈkuːpɒn] *n.*

菜式

菜系 style [staɪl] *n.*
汤 soup [suːp] *n.*
甜点 dessert [dɪˈzɜːt] *n.*
布丁 pudding [ˈpʊdɪŋ] *n.*
美味 delicacy [ˈdelɪkəsɪ] *n.*
剩菜 leftover [ˈleftəʊvə(r)] *n.*
素食主义者 vegetarian [ˌvedʒɪˈteərɪən] *n.*
家禽 poultry [ˈpəʊltrɪ] *n.*
香肠 sausage [ˈsɒsɪdʒ] *n.*
汉堡包 hamburger [ˈhæmbɜːgə(r)] *n.*
比萨饼 pizza [ˈpiːtsə] *n.*
炸薯条，炸土豆片 chips [tʃɪps] *n.*
奶酪 cheese [tʃiːz] *n.*
奶油 butter [ˈbʌtə(r)] *n.*
面包 bread [bred] *n.*
煎蛋卷 omelet [ˈɒmlɪt] *n.*
有营养的 nutritious [njuːˈtrɪʃəs] *adj.*
健康 health [helθ] *n.*
维生素 vitami [ˈvɪtəmɪn] *n.*
纤维 fiber [ˈfaɪbə(r)] *n.*
矿物质 mineral [ˈmɪnərəl] *n.*
脂肪 fat [fæt] *n.*

化肥 chemical ['kemɪkəl] *n.*
天然的 natural ['nætʃrəl] *adj.*
化肥 fertilizer ['fɜːtəˌlaɪzə] *n.*
意大利菜系 Italian specialities
美式食品 American favorites
法国菜 French food
广式菜 Cantonese cuisine
西餐 western food
西式自助餐 western buffet
主餐 main course
马铃薯泥 mashed potato
面包片 slice of bread
水煮蛋 boiled egg
煎蛋 fried egg
荷包蛋 poached egg
炒鸡蛋 scrambled egg
一口气 at one sitting
长胖 put on weight
快餐 fast food
均衡的饮食 balanced diet
油腻的食物 oily food
烹饪课 cooking class
各种各样的菜肴 various dishes
健康的食物 healthy food
家里做的饭 home-made meal
烹饪学校 cooking school

吃与喝

饮食 diet ['daɪət] *n.*
营养 nutrient ['njuːtrɪənt] *n.*
碳水化合物 carbohydrate [ˌkɑːbəʊ'haɪdreɪt] *n.*

矿物质 mineral ['mɪnərəl] *n.*

纤维 fiber ['faɪbə(r)] *n.*

消耗 consume [kən'sjuːm] *v.*

消化 digest [dɪ'dʒest] *v.*

吸收 absorb [əb'sɔːb] *v.*

咬 bite [baɪt] *v.*

嚼 chew [tʃuː] *v.*

咬 nibble ['nɪbl] *v.*

吞 swallow ['swɒləʊ] *v.*

食物金字塔 The Food Guide Pyramid

主要能量来源 major energy source

消化系统 digestive system

节食

饿 starve [stɑːv] *v.*

饥饿 hunger ['hʌŋgə(r)] *n.*

渴 thirst [θɜːst] *n.*

饥饿 starvation [stɑː'veɪʃn] *n.*

胃口 appetite ['æpɪtaɪt] *n.*

渴的 thirsty ['θəːstɪ] *adj.*

饮料 refreshment [rɪ'freʃmənt] *n.*

营养 nourish ['nʌrɪʃ] *v.*

量，份 portion ['pɔːʃn] *n.*

一道菜 course [kɔːs] *n.*

菜单 menu ['menjuː] *n.*

烹饪

炸，炒 fry [fraɪ] *v.*

煮 boil [bɔɪl] *v.*

煨 stew [stjuː] *v.*

蒸 steam [stiːm] *v.*

烤 bake [beɪk] *v.*

烧烤 barbecue ['bɑ:bɪkju:] *n.*

剥皮 peel [pi:l] *v.*

剁 chop [tʃɒp] *v.*

搅 stir [stɜ:(r)] *v.*

冷冻 freeze [fri:z] *v.*

状态

可吃的 eatable ['i:təbl] *adj.*

可吃的 edible ['edɪbl] *adj.*

可饮用的 drinkable ['drɪŋkəbl] *adj.*

消化的 digestible [dɪ'dʒestəbl] *adj.*

新鲜的 fresh [freʃ] *adj.*

生的 raw [rɔ:] *adj.*

过火的 overdone [,əʊvə'dʌn] *adj.*

七分熟的 underdone [,ʌndə'dʌn] *adj.*

硬的 tough [tʌf] *adj.*

软的 tender ['tendə(r)] *adj.*

开胃的 appetizing ['æpɪtaɪzɪŋ] *adj.*

好吃的 delicious [dɪ'lɪʃəs] *adj.*

好吃的 tasty ['teɪstɪ] *adj.*

没味的 tasteless ['teɪstlɪs] *adj.*

味道重的 pungent ['pʌndʒənt] *adj.*

辣的 spicy ['spaɪsɪ] *adj.*

美味的 delicious [dɪ'lɪʃəs] *adj.*

配料 ingredient [ɪn'gri:dɪənt] *n.*

熟的 well-done

让人留口水的 mouth-watering

泡菜罐子 pickle jar

菜谱 cookery book

水果

梨 pear [peər] *n.*

柑桔 tangerine [ˌtændʒə'riːn] *n.*

柑桔 mandarin ['mændərɪn] *n.*

橙 orange ['ɒrɪndʒ] *n.*

草莓 strawberry ['strɔːbrɪ] *n.*

菠萝 pineapple ['paɪnæpl] *n.*

李子 plum [plʌm] *n.*

荔枝 litchi [ˌlaɪ'tʃɪ] *n.*

桃子 peach [piːtʃ] *n.*

葡萄 grape [greɪp] *n.*

柠檬 lemon ['lemən] *n.*

樱桃 cherry ['tʃerɪ] *n.*

甘蔗 sugarcane ['ʃʊgərkeɪn] *n.*

西瓜 watermelon ['wɔːtərˌmelən] *n.*

柚子 grapefruit ['greɪpfruːt] *n.*

芒果 mango ['mæŋgəʊ] *n.*

梅子 plum [plʌm] *n.*

杏子 apricot ['eɪprɪkɒt] *n.*

山楂 hawthorn ['hɔːθɔːn] *n.*

榛子 hazelnut ['heɪzlnʌt] *n.*

椰子 coconut ['kəʊkənʌt] *n.*

枣 date [deɪt] *n.*

橄榄 olive ['ɒlɪv] *n.*

无花果 fig [fɪg] *n.*

杏仁 almond ['ɑːmənd] *n.*

栗子 chestnut ['tʃesnʌt] *n.*

坚果 nut [nʌt] *n.*

苹果核 apple core

苹果皮 apple skin

苹果汁 apple juice
梨核 pear core
无核桔 seedless orange
柑桔皮 orange peel
桔皮 tangerine skin
脐橙 naval orange
香蕉皮 banana skin
剥香蕉 peel a banana
葡萄核 grape stone
葡萄皮 grape skin
葡萄汁 grape juice
无籽西瓜 seedless watermelon
西瓜籽 watermelon seed
荸荠 water chestnut
板栗 Chinese chestnut
坚果壳 nut shell
坚果仁 nut meat

形容水果

成熟的 ripe [raɪp] *adj.*
未成熟的 unripe [ˌʌn'raɪp] *adj.*
嫩的 tender ['tendə(r)] *adj.*
脆的 crisp [krɪsp] *adj.*
多汁的 juicy ['dʒuːsɪ] *adj.*
光滑的 smooth [smuːð] *adj.*
软嫩的 soft [sɒft] *adj.*
松软的 spongy ['spʌndʒɪ] *adj.*
坚硬的 hard [hɑːd] *adj.*
甜的 sweet [swiːt] *adj.*
苦的 bitter ['bɪtə(r)] *adj.*

酸的 sour ['saʊə(r)] *adj.*
形状 shape [ʃeɪp] *n.*
早熟的 early-maturing
晚熟的 late-maturing
甜果 sweet fruit

肉类

猪肉 pork [pɔːk] *n.*
牛肉 beef [biːf] *n.*
牛肉 veal [viːl] *n.*
羊肉 mutton ['mʌtn]*n.*
羊肉 lamb [læm] *n.*
咸肉 bacon ['beɪkən] *n.*
肉丸 meatball ['miːtbɔːl] *n.*
腊肠 sausage ['sɒsɪdʒ] *n.*
鸡肉 chicken ['tʃɪkɪn] *n.*
鸭肉 duck [dʌk] *n.*
鹅肉 goose [guːs] *n.*
火鸡 turkey ['tɜːkɪ] *n.*
鸡 chicken ['tʃɪkɪn] *n.*
鸡翅 chicken wing
鸭 duck [dʌk] *n.*
鱼 fish [fɪʃ] *n.*
火腿 ham [hæm] *n.*
红肉 red meat
冻肉 frozen meat
鲜肉 fresh meat
肥肉 fat meat
瘦肉 lean meat
嫩肉 tender meat
白肉 white meat

海鲜

沙丁鱼 sardine [ˌsɑːˈdiːn] *n.*

小虾 shrimp [ʃrɪmp] *n.*

对虾 prawn [prɔːn] *n.*

牡蛎 oyster [ˈɔɪstə(r)] *n.*

章鱼 octopus [ˈɒktəpəs] *n.*

(海)蟹 crab [kræb] *n.*

墨鱼 inkfish [ˈɪŋkfɪʃ] *n.*

海带 kelp [kelp] *n.*

蜗牛 snail [sneɪl] *n.*

海螺 conch [kɒntʃ] *n.*

三文鱼 salmon [ˈsæmən] *n.*

海水鱼 sea fish

海蜇 jelly fish

海参 sea cucumber

河鲜 freshwater fish

鱼翅 shark's fin

冷盘

皮蛋 preserved duck egg

咸蛋 salted egg

血肠 black pudding / blood sausage

蔬菜

菠菜 spinach [ˈspɪnɪdʒ] *n.*

生菜 lettuce [ˈletɪs] *n.*

芹菜 celery [ˈselərɪ] *n.*

香菜 coriander [ˌkɒrɪˈændə(r)] *n.*

菜花 cauliflower [ˈkɒlɪflaʊə(r)]*n.*

西兰花 broccoli [ˈbrɒkəlɪ] *n.*

卷心菜 cabbage [ˈkæbɪdʒ] *n.*

豌豆 pea [piː] *n.*

黄瓜 cucumber [ˈkjuːkʌmbə(r)] *n.*

南瓜 pumpkin [ˈpʌmpkɪn] *n.*

蕃茄 tomato [təˈmɑːtəʊ] *n.*

茄子 eggplant [ˈegplɑːnt] *n.* (美)

茄子 aubergine [ˈəʊbəʒiːn] *n.* (英)

胡萝卜 carrot [ˈkærət] *n.*

芦笋 asparagus [əˈspærəgəs] *n.*

蘑菇 mushroom [ˈmʌʃruːm] *n.*

韭菜 leek [liːk] *n.*

蒜 garlic [ˈgɑːlɪk] *n.*

洋葱 onion [ˈʌnɪən] *n.*

小葱 spring onion

姜 ginger [ˈdʒɪndʒə(r)] *n.*

芸豆 kidney bean

刀豆 string bean

青椒 green pepper

辣椒 hot pepper

藕 lotus roots

竹笋 bamboo shoots

零食

饼干 biscuit [ˈbɪskɪt] *n.*

饼干 cracker [ˈkrækə(r)] *n.*

曲奇饼 cookie [ˈkʊkɪ] *n.*

水果蛋糕 fruitcake [ˈfruːtkeɪk] *n.*

水果蛋糕 tart [tɑːt] *n.*

华夫饼 waffle [ˈwɒfl] *n.*

热狗 hot dog

生日蛋糕 birthday cake

月饼 moon cake
糖果 candy ['kændɪ] *n.*
薯片 crisp [krɪsp] *n.*
葵花子 sunflower seeds

奶制品

冰淇淋 ice cream
奶油 cream [kriːm] *n.*
香草冰淇淋 vanilla ice cream
蛋卷冰淇淋 ice-cream cone
速溶咖啡 instant coffee
全脂牛奶 whole milk
脱脂牛奶 skim milk / nonfat milk
奶粉 milk powder
炼乳 condensed milk
奶酪 cheese [tʃiːz] *n.*
黄油 butter ['bʌtə(r)] *n.*

面粉

面团 dough [dəʊ] *n.*
煎饼 pancake ['pæŋkeɪk] *n.*
面条 pasta ['pæstə] *n.*
面条，挂面 noodle ['nuːdl] *n.*
通心粉 macaroni [ˌmækə'rəʊnɪ] *n.*
意大利面 spaghetti [spə'getɪ] *n.*
千层面 lasagna [lə'zænjə] *n.*

调味品

香料 spice [spaɪs] *n.*
盐 salt [sɔːlt] *n.*
醋 vinegar ['vɪnɪgə(r)] *n.*
酱油 sauce [sɔːs] *n.*

辣椒 pepper ['pepə(r)] *n.*

芥末 mustard ['mʌstəd] *n.*

黄油 butter ['bʌtə(r)] *n.*

调料 condiments ['kɒndɪmənts] *n.*

调料 seasoning ['siːzənɪŋ] *n.*

番茄酱 ketchup ['ketʃəp] *n.*

沙拉 salad ['sæləd] *n.*

香草 vanilla [və'nɪlə] *n.*

糖 sugar ['ʃʊgə(r)] *n.*

糖浆 syrup ['sɪrəp] *n.*

冰糖 sugar candy / rock candy

冰糖 candy ['kændɪ] *n.*

食油 cooking oil

油 oil [ɔɪl] *n.*

果酱 jam [dʒæm] *n.*

巧克力酱 chocolate spread

花生 peanut ['piːnʌt] *n.*

葡萄干 raisin ['reɪzn] *n.*

酱菜 pickle ['pɪkl] *n.*

沙拉酱 salad dressing

精制糖 refined sugar

方糖 cube sugar

精制油 refined oil

植物油 vegetable oil

豆油 bean oil

花生油 peanut oil

色拉油 salad oil

橄榄油 olive oil

麻油 sesame oil

方便食品 instant food
方便面 instant noodles
桔子酱 marmalade ['mɑːməleɪd] *n.*
番茄酱 tomato sauce
花生酱 peanut butter
芝麻酱 sesame paste
银耳 white fungus
黑木耳 black fungus
什锦酱菜 assorted pickles

饮料

可乐 colas ['kɒləs] *n.*
汽水 soda water
汽水 pop [pɒp] *n.*
柠檬汽水 lemonade [ˌleməˈneɪd] *n.*
柠檬汁 lemon juice
热饮 hot drink
冷饮 cold drink
酒精饮料 alcoholic drink
不含酒精饮料 non-alcoholic drink
果汁 fruit juice
苏打水 soda water
汤力水 tonic water
可口可乐 Coca-Cola
百事可乐 Pepsi-Cola
软性饮料 soft drink
矿泉水 mineral water
纯净水 pure water
橙汁 orange juice
茉莉花茶 jasmine tea

绿茶 green tea

红茶 black tea

雀巢咖啡 Nestle coffee

酒类

啤酒 beer [bɪə(r)] *n.*

啤酒 ale [eɪl] *n.*

白酒 alcohol ['ælkəhɒl] *n.*

白酒 liquor ['lɪkə(r)] *n.*

香槟酒 champagne [ʃæm'peɪn] *n.*

烈性酒 spirits ['spɪrɪts] *n.*

烈性酒 liquor ['lɪkə(r)] *n.*

威士忌酒 whisky ['wɪskɪ] *n.*

伏特加酒 vodka ['vɒdkə] *n.*

白兰地酒 brandy ['brændɪ] *n.*

鸡尾酒 cocktail ['kɒkteɪl] *n.*

法国白兰地 cognac ['kɒnjæk] *n.*

杜松子酒 gin [dʒɪn] *n.*

马爹利 martini [mɑː'tiːnɪ] *n.*

米酒 rice wine

红葡萄酒 red wine

白葡萄酒 white wine

绍兴酒 shaohsing wine

黄酒 yellow wine

高粱酒 Kaoliang spirit

厨房用具

餐具 cutlery ['kʌtlərɪ] *n.*

叉子 fork [fɔːk] *n.*

餐刀 knife [naɪf] *n.*

匙 spoon [spuːn] *n.*

茶匙 teaspoon ['tiːspuːn] *n.*
汤匙 soupspoon ['suːpspuːn] *n.*
筷子 chopsticks ['tʃɒpstɪks] *n.*
勺 ladle ['leɪdl] *n.*
沙锅 casserole ['kæsərəʊl] *n.*
茶壶 teapot ['tiːpɒt] *n.*
茶杯 teacup ['tiːkʌp] *n.*
漏斗 funnel ['fʌnl] *n.*
炒菜锅 frying pan
砧板 chopping board

scenery 景色

必备 海边 seaside ['siːsaɪd] *n.*
大陆 mainland ['meɪnlænd] *n.*
度假胜地 resort [rɪ'zɔːt] *n.*
目的地 destination [ˌdestɪ'neɪʃn] *n.*
呼吸 breathe [briːð] *v.*
纪念品 souvenir [ˌsuːvə'nɪə(r)] *n.*
兴旺的 prosperous ['prɒspərəs] *adj.*
交通 transportation [ˌtrænspɔː'teɪʃn] *n.*
文明 civilization [ˌsɪvəlaɪ'zeɪʃn] *n.*
景点 scenic spots
名胜古迹 historical sights
人文景观 artificial scenery
自然景观 natural landscape
微缩景区 miniature landscape
假日野营 holiday camp
野营胜地 camping resort
海滨休养地 seaside resort
公共海滨 public beach

私人海滨 private beach
海滨沙滩 sand beach
自然风景 natural beauties
著名旅游胜地 famous resort
自然景观 natural scene
和煦的微风 gentle breeze
壮观的事物 spectacular thing
花的芬芳 fragrance of flowers
外汇 foreign exchange
拓宽视野 broaden one's view
文化和习俗 cultures and customs
惊喜 pleasant surprise
假日旅馆 holiday inn
发展经济 develop the economy
被破坏 be spoiled

season 季节

Tips: 适用于 your favorite season (你最喜爱的季节)，在描述假期、家乡时，可以提及下面的活动。

必备 各式活动 various activities
去海边 go to the seaside
吃烧烤 enjoy barbeque
沙滩排球 beach volleyball
爬山 go climbing
划船 go boating
躺在沙滩上 lie on the beach
享受阳光 enjoy the sunshine
喜欢花儿绽放 enjoy the flowers blooming
充满活力和愉快的 energetic and sunny
去乡下 go to the countryside

绿色食品 organic food
玩得愉快 have fun
去露营 go camping
短途旅行 go for a trip
待在小木屋里 stay in the hut
听鸟儿发出的唧唧声 listen to the chirping of birds
远足 go outing
建筑风格 construction style
少数民族 minority nationalities
多彩的夜生活 colorful nightlife
享受娱乐 enjoy entertainment

shopping 购物

Tips: 适用于 department store (商店)、an open-air market (市场)、something you bought that made you angry (让你不满意的东西)、a thing you lost (你丢失的东西)、present (礼物) 和 something you want to save money to buy (你想攒钱买的东西)。

必备 情感 emotion [ɪ'məʊʃn] *n.*
衣物 clothes [kləʊðz] *n.*
书籍 book [bʊk] *n.*
玩具 toy [tɔɪ] *n.*
小器具 gadget ['gædʒɪt] *n.*
感受和关注 feeling and concern
花和化妆品 flowers or cosmetics
精致地包装礼物 pack gifts elegantly
超市 supermarket ['suːpəmɑːkɪt] *n.*
超市 hypermarket ['haɪpəmɑːkɪt] *n.*
集市摊位 stall [stɔːl] *n.*
书报亭 kiosk ['kiːɒsk] *n.*
精品店 boutique [buː'tiːk] *n.*

市场 market ['mɑːkɪt] *n.*

大集市 bazaar [bə'zɑː(r)] *n.*

拍卖 auction ['ɔːkʃn] *n.*

花店 florist ['flɒrɪst] *n.*

购物者 shopper ['ʃɒpə] *n.*

顾客 customer ['kʌstəmə(r)] *n.*

店主 shopkeeper ['ʃɒpkiːpə(r)] *n.*

售货员 salesman ['seɪlzmən]

柜台 counter ['kaʊntə(r)] *n.*

架子 shelf [ʃelf] *n.*

购物车 trolley ['trɒlɪ] *n.*

购物推车 cart [kɑːt] *n.*

运动服 sportswear ['spɔːtswɪə] *n.*

酸奶 yogurt ['jɒgət] *n.*

洗发水 shampoo [ʃæm'puː] *n.*

商场 department store

连锁店 chain store

购物中心 shopping center

干货 dry goods

五金店 hardware store

只看不买 window shopping

淘货品 bargain shopping

购物日 shopping day

购物清单 shopping list

购物袋 shopping bag

购物篮 shopping basket

售货员 shop assistant

收款台 cash-desk

收款台 checkout ['tʃekaʊt] *n.*

浪费时间 a waste of time
获取建议 ask for advice
葵花子 sunflower seeds
商业中心 shopping mall
销售助理 sales assistants
促销产品 promote products
降低价格 lower prices
最新消息 latest information
数码相机 digital camera
售后服务 post-sale service
诱人且时髦的 cute and fashionable
生活标准 living standard
各种品牌 various brands
商店助理 shop assistants
冷漠傲慢的 indifferent and arrogant

价格

贵的 high [haɪ] *adj.*
昂贵的 expensive [ɪk'spensɪv] *adj.*
昂贵的 costly ['kɒstlɪ] *adj.*
便宜的 cheap [tʃiːp] *adj.*
免费的 free [friː] *adj.*
便宜的 low [ləʊ] *adj.*
不贵的 inexpensive [ˌɪnɪk'spensɪv] *adj.*
经济实惠的 economical [ˌiːkə'nɒmɪkl] *adj.*
有价值的 valuable ['væljʊəbl] *adj.*
珍贵的 precious ['preʃəs] *adj.*
无价的 priceless ['praɪslɪs] *adj.*
便宜物品 a bargain
处理价 reduced price / bargain price

售价高 sell at a high price

售价低 sell at a low price

分量准足 give full weight

服务

必备

短斤缺两 give short weight

声誉 reputation [ˌrepjʊ'teɪʃn] *n.*

对雇员要求严格 strict with the employees

做出努力 make efforts

制定一些政策 set some policies

监督或者引导贸易的发展 monitor or guide the development of the commerce

全球视角 global view

获得更好的服务 get better service

投诉 make a complaint

有更多的顾客 have more customers

负面影响 negative effect

对他们的员工制定规章制度 make rules and regulations for their employees

被监督 be supervised

琐碎的错误 trivial mistake

耐心和特殊策略 patience and special strategies

机械产品 mechanic products

组装线 assembly line

容忍差劲的服务 tolerate the bad service

严格的法律 strict law

虐待顾客 mistreat consumers

保证他们的产品 guarantee their products

商店装潢

选记

展示台 showcase ['ʃəʊkeɪs] *n.*

杂货店 grocer ['grəʊsə(r)] *n.*

杂货店 greengrocer ['gri:ngrəʊsə(r)] *n.*

面包店 baker ['beɪkə] *n.*

香烟店 tobacconist [tə'bækənɪst] *n.*

药房 pharmacist ['fɑ:məsɪst] *n.*

药店 drugstore ['drʌgstɔ:(r)] *n.*

商店门脸 shop front

商店橱窗 shop window

糖果店 sweet shop

货品

选记 冒牌货 fake [feɪk] *n.*

冒牌货 counterfeit goods

玻璃制品 glassware ['glɑ:sweə] *n.*

搪瓷器皿 enamelware [ɪ'næml,weə] *n.*

文具 stationery ['steɪʃənrɪ] *n.*

照相机 camera ['kæmərə] *n.*

扇子 fan [fæn] *n.*

打火机 lighter ['laɪtə] *n.*

花瓶 flower vase

手套 gloves [glʌvz] *n.*

连指手套 mitten ['mɪtn] *n.*

雨伞 umbrella [ʌm'brelə] *n.*

雨衣 raincoat ['reɪnkəʊt] *n.*

针 needle ['ni:dl] *n.*

线 thread [θred] *n.*

剪刀 scissors ['sɪzəz] *n.*

扫帚 broom [bru:m] *n.*

冰箱 refrigerator [rɪ'frɪdʒəreɪtə] *n.*

冰箱 fridge [frɪdʒ] *n.*

电筒 torch [tɔːtʃ] *n.*

电筒 flashlight [ˈflæʃlaɪt] *n.*

电池 battery [ˈbætrɪ] *n.*

电池 cell [sel] *n.*

蜡烛 candle [ˈkændl] *n.*

窗帘 curtain [ˈkɜːtn] *n.*

百叶窗 blind [blaɪnd] *n.*

地毯 carpet [ˈkɑːpɪt] *n.*

地毯 rug [rʌg] *n.*

门垫 mat [mæt] *n.*

温度计 thermometer [θəˈmɒmɪtə(r)] *n.*

摇篮 cradle [ˈkreɪdl] *n.*

洗涤剂 detergent [dɪˈtɜːdʒənt] *n.*

洗衣板 washboard [ˈwɒʃbɔːd] *n.*

水桶 pail [peɪl] *n.*

电吹风 hairdryer [ˈheəˌdraɪə] *n.*

化妆品 cosmetic [kɒzˈmetɪk] *n.*

香水 perfume [ˈpɜːfjuːm] *n.*

口红 lipstick [ˈlɪpˌstɪk] *n.*

眼线笔 eyeliner [ˈaɪˌlaɪnə] *n.*

染发剂 hairdye [ˈheədaɪ] *n.*

浴衣 bathrobe [ˈbɑːθrəʊb] *n.*

浴缸 bathtub [ˈbɑːθtʌb] *n.*

毛巾 towel [ˈtaʊəl] *n.*

牙刷 toothbrush [ˈtuːθbrʌʃ] *n.*

牙膏 toothpaste [ˈtuːθpeɪst] *n.*

镜子 mirror [ˈmɪrə] *n.*

梳子 comb [kəʊm] *n.*

泳衣 swimsuit [ˈswɪmsuːt] *n.*

救生圈 life buoy
箱子 suitcase ['suːtkeɪs] *n.*
不锈钢制的 stainless ['steɪnlɪs] *adj.*
文具商 stationer ['steɪʃnə] *n.*
画笔 paintbrush ['peɪntbrʌʃ] *n.*
蜡笔 crayon ['kreɪən] *n.*
笔记本 notebook ['nəʊtbʊk] *n.*
浆糊 glue [gluː] *n.*
算盘 abacus ['æbəkəs] *n.*
计算器 calculator ['kælkjʊleɪtə] *n.*
大头针 pin [pɪn] *n.*
文件夹 file [faɪl] *n.*
订书钉 staple ['steɪpl] *n.*
订书机 stapler ['steɪplə] *n.*
沙漏 hourglass ['aʊglɑːs] *n.*
沙漏 sandglass ['sændglɑːs] *n.*
日晷 sundial ['sʌndaɪəl] *n.*
计时机 chronometer [krə'nɒmɪtə(r)] *n.*
秒表 stopwatch [stɒpwɒtʃ] *n.*
定时器 timer ['taɪmə] *n.*
钟摆 pendulum ['pendjʊləm] *n.*
日历 calendar ['kælɪndə] *n.*
锁 lock [lɒk] *n.*
门闩 latch [lætʃ] *n.*
锁孔 keyhole ['kiːhəʊl] *n.*
球形把手 knob [nɒb] *n.*
钳子 pliers ['plaɪəz] *n.*
锯子 saw [sɔː] *n.*
锉刀 file [faɪl] *n.*

塑料制品 plastic goods
塑料制品 plastics ['plæstɪks] n.
时兴货 popular articles
名牌货 name brand
最新产品 latest product
传统商品 traditional goods
耐用品 durable goods
花哨商品 fancy goods
廉价商品部 bargain basement
美术用品 art supplies
棉织品 cotton textiles / cotton fabrics
毛织品 woollen textiles / woollen fabrics
丝织品 silk fabrics
针织品 knit goods
针织品 knitwear ['nɪtweə] n.
钩针织品 crotchet work
亚麻织品 linen fabrics
乐器 musical instrument
童装 children's wear
橡胶手套 rubber gloves
指甲钳 nail clipper
卫生用具 sanitary utensils
干电池 dry battery
太阳能电池 solar cell
充电电池 rechargeable battery
电池充电器 battery charger
台灯 table lamp / desk lamp / reading lamp
吊灯 ceiling lamp
壁灯 wall lamp

床头灯 bedside lamp
灯泡 electric bulb
日光灯 fluorescent lamp
洗衣机 washing machine
洗衣粉 washing powder
餐巾纸 paper napkin
香粉 face powder
粉扑 powder puff
眉笔 eyebrow pencil
指甲油 nail polish
洁肤霜 cleansing cream
爽身粉 talcum powder
发刷 hair brush
泳衣 swimming costume
泳裤 swimming trunks
泳帽 swimming cap
帆布箱 canvas suitcase
皮箱 leather suitcase
旅行箱 travelling case
开罐刀 can opener
电炉 electric stove
电熨斗 electric iron
电热毯 electric blanket
钢笔 fountain pen
毛笔 writing brush
圆珠笔 ball-point pen / ball pen
活动铅笔 propelling pencil
签名笔 felt-tip pen
荧光笔 high-lighter

文房四宝 four treasures of the study
日记本 diary book
活页本 loose-leaf note book
改正笔 correction pen
改正液 correction fluid
文具盒 stationery case
回形针 paper clip
图钉 drawing pin
透明胶 scotch tape
双面胶 twin adhesive
昆虫标本 insect specimen
地球仪 terrestrial globe
闹钟 alarm clock
落地挂钟 grandfather clock
石英钟 quartz clock
座钟 desk clock / table clock
挂钟 wall clock
石英表 quartz watch
名贵表 luxurious watches
金表 gold watch
对表 a pair of watches
时装表 fancy watch
怀表 pocket watch
电子表 digital watch
防水表 waterproof watch
表链 watch chain
秒针 second hand
分针 minute hand
安全锁 safety lock

丁字尺 T-square

折叠刀 folding knife

果园用大剪刀 garden shears

电剃刀 electric razor

show / performance 表演

必备 生日晚会表演 birthday party shows

才艺表演 talent shows

剧院节目 theatrical production

户外表演 outdoor shows

餐厅表演 restaurant shows

马戏表演 circus performance

skill 技能

Tips: 适用于 something you are good at 和 your favorite clothes or jewelry (最喜爱的服装或珠宝)。

必备 竞争 competition [ˌkɒmpəˈtɪʃn] *n.*

生存 survive [səˈvaɪv] *v.*

才能 talent [ˈtælənt] *n.*

动机 motivation [ˌməʊtɪˈveɪʃn] *n.*

潜力 potential [pəˈtenʃl] *n.*

管理技能 management skill

快速的反应 quick response

拓宽视野 widen sights

开发智力 develop children's intelligence

好成绩 high academic records

忽略其他技能 neglect other skills

个人兴趣 personal interest

有更强的信心 have more confidence

有很强的动力 have strong drive

给予孩子们鼓励 give children encouragement
指导和支持 guidance and support
技术能力 technical and technological skills
组织能力 ability to organize
劝说能力 persuasive skills
交际技能 communication skills

something you lost 失物

必备 失物招领处 lost and found
犯罪率 crime rate
盗窃 theft [θeft] *n.*
扒手 pick-pocket
顺手牵羊的人 shop lifter
小偷 thief [θiːf] *n.*

sports 运动

Tips: 适用于 your favorite sports (最喜爱的体育节目) 和 a sports event (你看过的体育赛事)。

必备 流行 popularity [ˌpɒpjʊ'lærətɪ] *n.*
勇气 courage ['kʌrɪdʒ] *n.*
社团 community [kə'mjuːnɪtɪ] *n.*
运动场 stadium ['steɪdɪəm] *n.*
竞争者 contestant [kən'testənt] *n.*
有氧运动 aerobics [eə'rəʊbɪks] *n.*
瑜珈 yoga ['jəʊgə] *n.*
跑步机 treadmill ['tredmɪl] *n.*
滚轴溜冰 rollerblading ['rəʊləbleɪdɪŋ] *n.*
去慢跑 go jogging
激烈的竞争 fierce competition
展示最好的一面 show their best
强劲的体格 strong physique

体形训练 fitness training
训练课程 training courses
提前 in advance
赛车 car racing
体育事件 sports events
分享利润 share the profits
保持良好体形 keep good shape
有强壮的身体 have strong body
现代生活 modern life
极限运动 X-games
攀岩 rocking climbing
感到轻松振作 feel relaxed and refreshed

比赛

锦标赛 tournament ['tʊənəmənt] *n.*
业余选手 amateur ['æmətə(r)] *n.*
健身 bodybuilding ['bɒdɪbɪldɪŋ] *n.*
冠军地位，冠军赛，锦标赛 championship ['tʃæmpɪənʃɪp] *n.*
冠军 champion ['tʃæmpɪən] *n.*
奖牌 medal ['medl] *n.*
裁判 referee [ˌrefə'riː] *n.*
裁判 umpire ['ʌmpaɪə(r)] *n.*
秒表 stopwatch ['stɒpwɒtʃ] *n.*
经纪人 manager ['mænɪdʒə(r)] *n.*
教练，技术指导 instructor [ɪn'strʌktə(r)] *n.*
领队 guide [gaɪd] *n.*
助理教练 trainer ['treɪnə(r)] *n.*
运动员 contestant [kən'testənt] *n.*
运动员 competitor [kəm'petɪtə(r)] *n.*
运动员 player ['pleɪə(r)] *n.*

职业运动员 professional [prə'feʃənl] *n.*
纪录 record ['rekɔːd] *n.*
圈 ring [rɪŋ] *n.*
场地 ground [graʊnd] *n.*
场地 field [fiːld] *n.*
(足球、橄榄球) 场地 pitch [pɪtʃ] *n.*
网球场 court [kɔːt] *n.*
国际比赛 international game
公开赛 open tournament
表演赛 exhibition match
邀请赛 invitational match
友谊赛 friendly match
安慰赛 consolation match
世界冠军地位 world championship
铜牌 bronze medal
银牌 silver medal
金牌 gold medal
奥林匹克火炬 Olympic torch
奥运村 Olympic village
开幕式 opening ceremony
接力赛 relay race
纪录创造者 record holder
奥林匹克运动会 Olympic Games
奥林匹克运动会 Olympics [ə'lɪmpɪks] *n.*
冬季奥林匹克运动会 Winter Olympics

游泳

Tips: 适用于 your favorite swimming place (最喜爱的游泳场所)。
游泳 swimming ['swɪmɪŋ] *n.*
比基尼 bikini [bɪ'kiːnɪ] *n.*

跳水 diving ['daɪvɪŋ] *n.*
充满活力的 kicking ['kɪkɪŋ] *adj.*
潜水镜 hydroscope ['haɪdrəʊskəʊp] *n.*
冲浪运动 surfing ['sɜːfɪŋ] *n.*
冲浪运动员 surfrider ['sɜːfˌraɪdə(r)] *n.*
冲浪运动员 surfer ['sɜːfə(r)] *n.*
冲浪板 surfboard ['sɜːfbɔːd] *n.*
游泳池 swimming pool
室外游泳池 open-air pool
室内游泳池 indoor pool
游泳设备 swimming facilities
更衣室 changing room
更衣室 locker room
更衣室 dressing room
游泳帽 swimming trunks
游泳衣 swimming suit
泳道 swim lane
跳台 diving tower
跳台 platform ['plætfɔːm] *n.*
自由泳 free style
蛙泳 breast stroke
海豚式 dolphin stroke
仰泳 back stroke
蝶泳 butterfly stroke
侧泳 side stroke
狗刨式 dog paddle
潜泳 underwater swimming
救生圈 life buoy
摩托艇比赛 motor-boat race

滑水 water skiing

滑水橇 water ski

滑水运动员 water-skier

冬季运动

滑冰运动 skating ['skeɪtɪŋ] *n.*

雪橇 sleigh [sleɪ] *n.*

旱冰鞋 roller skates

花样滑冰 figure skating

轮式滑冰 roller skating

足球

足球 football ['fʊtbɔːl] *n.*

足球 soccer ['sɒkə(r)] *n.*

球门 goal [gəʊl] *n.*

撞人 charging ['tʃɑːdʒɪŋ] *n.*

替补队员 bench [bentʃ] *n.*

队友 teammate ['tiːmmeɪt] *n.*

中卫 halfback ['hɑːfbæk] *n.*

教练 coach [kəʊtʃ] *n.*

教练 trainer ['treɪnə] *n.*

巡边员 linesman ['laɪnzmən] *n.*

队长 captain ['kæptɪn] *n.*

决赛 final ['faɪnl] *n.*

足球场 football field

球门网 goal net

球门柱 goal post

中线 halfway line

罚球区 penalty area

罚球点 penalty spot

罚任意球 free kick

罚点球 penalty kick
角球区 corner kick area
角旗 corner flag
角球 corner ball
开球 kick-off
传球 pass the ball
长传 long passing
短传 short passing
头顶传球 head passing
脚内侧传球 inside foot passing
脚外侧传球 outside foot passing
接球 take a pass
射门 goal shooting
假动作 make a feint
假动作 feinting ['feɪntɪŋ] *n.*
越位 off-side
合法撞人 fair charge
肩膀撞人 shoulder charge
危险动作 dangerous play
职业队 professional team
业余队 amateur team
足球队员 football player
出场队员 quarters player
左翼 left wing
右翼 right wing
左前锋 left forward
右前锋 right forward
中锋 centre forward
左内锋 inside left forward

右内锋 inside right forward

左边锋 outside left forward

右边锋 outside right forward

左中卫 left halfback

右中卫 right halfback

中卫 centre halfback

后卫 full back

上半时 first half

下半时 second half

领队 team manager

预赛 trial match

预赛 preliminary [prɪˈlɪmɪnərɪ] *n.*

半决赛 semi-final

赛前练习 warming-up practice

足球袜 football sock

网球

网球运动 tennis [ˈtenɪs] *n.*

球拍 racket [ˈrækɪt] *n.*

斜线球 crosscourt [ˈkrɒskɔːt] *n.*

抽球 smash [smæʃ] *n.*

削球 cut [kʌt] *n.*

旋转球 spin [spɪn] *v.*

截击空中球 volley [ˈvɒlɪ] *n.*

落网球 net [net] *n.*

重发球 let [let] *v.*

机会球 fluke [fluːk] *n.*

机会球 set-up

机会球 easy [ˈiːzɪ] *n.*

局 game [geɪm] *n.*

盘 set [set] *n.*
局末平分，盘末平局 deuce [djuːs] *n.*
发球员 server [ˈsɜːvə(r)] *n.*
接球员 receiver [rɪˈsiːvə(r)] *n.*
打出边线的 (球) wide [waɪd] *adj.*
草地网球运动 lawn tennis
草地网球场 grass court
球拍夹 racket press
球拍夹 string [strɪŋ] *n.*
(球拍的) 弦 gut [gʌt] *n.*
触线球 line ball
底线球 baseline ball
边线球 sideline ball
直线球 straight ball
边线直线球 down-the-line shot
低球 low ball
长球 long shot
短球 short shot
跃起抽球 jump smash
抽低球 low drive
低截球 low volley
深球 deep ball
重球 heavy ball
平击球 flat stroke
平抽球 flat drive
击触地球 ground stroke
高球扣杀 overhead smash
高球扣杀 overhand smash
一平 fifteen all

二平 thirty all
三平 forty all
一方得零分的一局 love game
双误，两次发球失误 double fault
发球线 service line
前场 fore court
后场 back court
中点 centre mark
网球场 tennis court

篮球

篮球 basketball ['bɑːskɪtbɔːl] *n.*
篮架 basket support
界线 boundary line
边线 side line
“三秒” "three seconds"
技术犯规 technical offence
双方犯规 double foul
暂停 time-out
换人 removal of player / change of player
加时比赛 extra game
延长比赛 extra period
投篮不中 miss the basket
投篮不准 inaccurate shooting

其他运动

排球 volleyball ['vɒlɪbɔːl] *n.*
排球场 volleyball court
排球网 volleyball net
发球区 service area
攻击区 attack area

橄榄球 rugby ['rʌgbɪ] *n.*

护面罩 mask [mɑːsk] *n.*

护面罩 helmet ['helmɪt] *n.*

羽毛球 badminton ['bædmɪntən] *n.*

羽毛球 shuttlecock ['ʃʌtlkɒk] *n.*

羽毛球拍 racket ['rækɪt] *n.*

高尔夫球 golf [gɒlf] *n.*

曲棍球 hockey ['hɒkɪ] *n.*

台球 billiards ['bɪlɪədz] *n.*

板球 cricket ['krɪkɪt] *n.*

槌球 croquet ['krəʊkeɪ] *n.*

马球 polo ['pəʊləʊ] *n.*

棒球场 baseball field

边线 touch line

头盔 football helmet

羽毛球场 badminton court

高尔夫球场 golf course

乒乓球 table tennis

冰球 ice hockey

水球 water polo

马球运动员 polo player

预赛 trials ['traɪəlz] *n.*

标枪 javelin (throw)

铁饼 discus (throw)

马拉松赛跑 marathon (race)

跨栏赛跑 hurdles ['hɜːdlz] *n.*

跨栏赛跑 hurdle race

终点 finish ['fɪnɪʃ] *n.*

跑道 track [træk] *n.*

体操 gymnastics [dʒɪm'næstɪks] *n.*

体操运动员 gymnast ['dʒɪmnæst] *n.*

吊环 rings [rɪŋz] *n.*

吊环 swinging rings

跳板 springboard ['sprɪŋbɔːd] *n.*

难度 difficulty ['dɪfɪkəltɪ] *n.*

协调 harmony ['hɑːmənɪ] *n.*

优美 elegance ['elɪgəns] *n.*

准确 accuracy ['ækjʊrəsɪ] *n.*

击剑 fencing ['fensɪŋ] *n.*

面具 mask [mɑːsk] *n.*

面具 helmet ['helmɪt] *n.*

拳击 boxing ['bɒksɪŋ] *n.*

空手道 karate [kə'rɑːtɪ] *n.*

拳击手 boxer ['bɒksə] *n.*

自行车比赛 cycling ['saɪklɪŋ] *n.*

射击 shooting ['ʃuːtɪŋ] *n.*

射箭 archery ['ɑːtʃərɪ] *n.*

滑翔 gliding ['glaɪdɪŋ] *n.*

摔跤 wrestling ['reslɪŋ] *n.*

摔角运动员 wrestler ['reslə] *n.*

相扑 sumo ['suːməʊ] *n.*

柔道 judo ['dʒuːdəʊ] *n.*

跳伞运动员 parachutist ['pærəʃuːtɪst] *n.*

武术 martial arts

武术 wushu ['wuː'ʃuː] *n.*

跳伞 parachute jumping

跳伞 parachuting ['pærəʃuːtɪŋ] *n.*

田径运动 track & field events

田赛 field events
径赛 track events
运动会 sports meet
跳高 high jump
跳远 broad jump / long jump
障碍赛跑 obstacle race
竞走 walking race
起跑线 starting line
终点带 finishing tape
单杠 horizontal bar
双杠 parallel bars
高低杠 uneven bars
平衡木 balance beam
跳马 vaulting horse
鞍马 pommelled horse
跳箱 box horse
自由体操 free exercise / floor exercise
健美操 fitness exercise / bodybuilding exercise
藤圈操 hoop exercise
哑铃操 dumb-bell exercise
徒手操 free-hand exercise
规定动作 compulsory exrercise
自选动作 optional exercise
垫上运动 mat exercise
俯卧撑 push-up
满分 full score
加分 bonus point
剑师 fencing master
击剑教练 fencing instructor

泰国拳 Thai boxing

公路自行车比赛 road cycling

赛场自行车比赛 track cycling

自由式摔跤 free-style wrestling

古典式摔跤 traditional wrestling

举重 weight-lifting

棋赛 chess competition

棋盘 chess board

保龄球、台球

选记 保龄球 bowling ['bəʊlɪŋ] *n.*

玩保龄球的人 bowler ['bəʊlə] *n.*

保龄球用的圆球 bowl [bəʊl] *n.*

保龄球道 bowling alley

十柱戏 tenpin bowling

九柱戏 ninepins ['naɪnpɪnz] *n.*

台球房 billiard room

台球房 poolroom ['puːlrʊm] *n.*

台球台 billiard table

台球盘面绿呢 billiard cloth

打台球者 billiard player

纸牌

选记 玩牌室 cardroom ['kɑːdrʊm] *n.*

纸牌 card [kɑːd] *n.*

玩牌的人 cardplayer ['kɑːdˌpleɪə] *n.*

黑桃 spade [speɪd] *n.*

红桃 heart [hɑːt] *n.*

方块 diamond ['daɪəmənd] *n.*

梅花 club [klʌb] *n.*

王牌 trump [trʌmp] *n.*

赢家 winner ['wɪnə] *n.*

洗牌 shuffle ['ʃʌfl] *n.*

洗牌者 shuffler ['ʃʌflə] *n.*

发牌 deal [diːl] *n.*

发牌者 dealer ['diːlə] *n.*

发牌盒 dealing box

桥牌 bridge [brɪdʒ] *n.*

桥牌戏中的叫牌 bidding ['bɪdɪŋ] *n.*

打桥牌 play bridge

一副纸牌 a pack of cards

纸牌戏 card-game

象棋

选 记 棋室 chessroom ['tʃesruːm] *n.*

国际象棋 chess [tʃes] *n.*

国际象棋 the game of chess

国际象棋棋子 chessman ['tʃesmæn] *n.*

国际象棋中的王 king [kɪŋ] *n.*

国际象棋中的后 queen [kwiːn] *n.*

国际象棋中的象 bishop ['bɪʃəp] *n.*

国际象棋中的车 rook [rʊk] *n.*

国际象棋中的车 castle ['kɑːsl] *n.*

国际象棋中的兵 pawn [pɔːn] *n.*

下棋者 chess player

棋迷 chess fan

白子 white piece

黑子 black piece

中国象棋 Chinese Chess

跳棋

选 记 跳棋 halma ['hælmə] *n.*

跳棋 the game of halma

国际跳棋 draughts [drɑːfts] *n.*

国际跳棋 the game of draughts

西洋跳棋 chequers ['tʃekəz] *n.*

西洋跳棋 checkers ['tʃekəz] *n.*

多米诺骨牌戏 dominoes ['dɒmɪnəʊs] *n.*

麻将 mahjong [ˌmɑː'dʒɒŋ] *n.*

中国跳棋 Chinese checkers

玩掷骰游戏 play dice

打麻将 play mahjong

station 车站

必备 行李 baggage ['bægɪdʒ] *n.*

行李 luggage ['lʌgɪdʒ] *n.*

行李寄存处 baggageroom ['bægɪdʒruːm] *n.*

行李寄存处 checkroom ['tʃekruːm] *n.*

时刻表 timetable ['taɪmteɪbl] *n.*

地铁代用币 token ['təʊkən] *n.*

检票员 gateman ['geɪtmæn] *n.*

站长 stationmaster ['steɪʃnˌmɑːstə(r)] *n.*

搬运工 porter ['pɔːtə(r)] *n.*

列车长 captain ['kæptɪn] *n.*

晚点 late [leɪt] *adv.*

晚点 behind schedule

到达站 destination [ˌdestɪ'neɪʃn] *n.*

终点站 terminal ['tɜːmɪnl] *n.*

晕火车的 trainsick ['treɪnsɪk] *adj.*

枢纽站 junction ['dʒʌŋkʃn] *n.*

地铁 subway ['sʌbweɪ] *n.*

地铁 underground railway

地铁 tube [tju:b] *n.*

车厢 railroad car

车厢 carriage ['kærɪdʒ] *n.*

车厢 compartment [kəm'pɑ:tmənt] *n.*

普通车厢 coach [kəʊtʃ] *n.*

过道 corridor ['kɒrɪdɔ:(r)] *n.*

卧铺车 sleeping car

卧铺车 sleeper ['sli:pə(r)] *n.*

铺位 bunk [bʌŋk] *n.*

软卧 carriage ['kærɪdʒ] *n.*

软卧 coach [kəʊtʃ] *n.*

电车 tramcar ['træmkɑ:(r)] *n.*

保险杠 bumper ['bʌmpə(r)] *n.*

前灯 headlight ['hedlaɪt] *n.*

反光灯 spotlight ['spɒtlaɪt] *n.*

散热器 radiator ['reɪdɪeɪtə(r)] *n.*

码头 dock [dɒk] *n.*

独木舟 canoe [kə'nu:] *n.*

木筏 raft [rɑ:ft] *n.*

划艇，小舟 rowboat ['rəʊbəʊt] *n.*

舢舨 sampan ['sæmpæn] *n.*

气垫船 air-cushion vehicle

汽艇 motorboat ['məʊtə(r)bəʊt] *n.*

游艇 yacht [jɒt] *n.*

邮轮 liner ['laɪnə] *n.*

全体船员 crew [kru:] *n.*

船长 captain ['kæptɪn] *n.*

副官 mate [meɪt] *n.*

舵手 quartermaster ['kwɔ:tə(r)ˌmɑ:stə(r)] *n.*

飞机场 airport ['eə(r)pɔːt] *n.*
直升飞机 helicopter ['helɪkɒptə(r)] *n.*
跑道 runway ['rʌnweɪ] *n.*
升降机 elevator ['elɪveɪtə(r)] *n.*
停机坪 apron ['eɪprən] *n.*
航空公司 airlines ['eə(r)laɪnz] *n.*
机组成员 crewman ['kruːmən] *n.*
驾驶员 pilot ['paɪlət] *n.*
机长 captain ['kæptɪn] *n.*
副驾驶员 co-pilot [ˌkəʊ'paɪlət] *n.*
同座乘客 seatmate ['siːtmeɪt] *n.*
着陆 land [lænd] *v.*
晕机的 airsick ['eə(r)sɪk] *adj.*
候车室 waiting room
铁路站台 railway platform
下客站台 arrival platform
发车站台 departure platform
自动扶梯 travelling staircase
随身行李 personal luggage
超重行李 excess luggage
托运的行李 checked baggage
行李标签 luggage tag
行李房 luggage compartment
行李寄存证 baggage check
失物招领处 lost and found office
车站茶点室 refreshment room
车站指示牌 train indicator
单程票 one-way ticket / single ticket
往返票 round-trip ticket / return ticket

快车票 express ticket
卧铺票 berth ticket
定期车票 commuter's ticket
定期车票 season ticket
站台票 platform ticket
检票口 ticket gate
查票 examine tickets
查票员 ticket inspector
车站全体职员 station staff
开进车站 pull into the station
开出车站 pull out of the station
到达时间 time of arrival
开车时间 time of departure
准点 on schedule
订硬席票 book a hard seat
订卧铺票 book a berth
误车 miss a train
逃票乘火车 ride the rails
城市间的高速列车 metro-liner
国际列车 international train
特快列车 limited express train
直达列车 through train
市郊往返列车 commuter train
高速列车 bullet train
专列 special train
游览车 observation car
硬席 hard seat
靠通道的座位 aisle seat
靠窗座位 window seat

上铺 upper berth
下铺 lower berth
卧铺 sleeping berth
硬席卧铺 hard sleeper
餐车 dining-car / buffet car
公交公司 public transport company
公共交通 public transport
公交线路 bus line
双层公共汽车 double-decker bus
单层公共汽车 single-decker
有轨电车 trolley bus
市内公交车 cross-town bus
长途客车 long-distance bus
高峰车 rush hour bus
夜间车 night bus
头班车 first bus
末班车 last bus
无人售票车 one-man bus
游览车 sightseeing bus
未载客的出租车 deadhead cab
没乘上车 miss the bus
汽车代用币 bus token
逃票 jump the bus
高峰时间交通 peak traffic
交通拥挤时间 rush hour
上下班交通 commutation
交通堵塞 traffic jam
交通事故 traffic accident
发动引擎 start the engine

换档 shift gears
踩油门 step on the accelerator
刹车 step on the brake
加速 speed up
减速 slow down
急刹车 hit the brakes
左转 turn left
右转 turn right
掉头 make a U-turn
爆胎 have a flat tire
换胎 change the tire
停车 park the car
抛锚 break down
后座 back seat
汽车牌照 license plate
备用轮胎 spare tire
驾驶员座位 driver's seat
乘客座位 passenger seat
游览艇 cabin cruiser
客轮 passenger ship
远洋客轮 ocean liner
集装箱船 container ship
客舱 passenger cabin
大副 first mate
二副 second mate
三副 third mate
热气球 hot air balloon
超音速运输机 supersonic transport aircraft
一等舱 first class seating

二等舱 tourist class seating
经济客舱 economy class seating
安全带 seat belt
救生背心 life vest
氧气面罩 oxygen mask
救生伞 survival parachute
航空集散站 air terminal
航行灯 running light
指挥塔台 control tower
免费携带行李限额 free luggage allowance
班次 flight number
机械师 flight engineer
空中小姐 air hostess
起飞 take off
强迫降落 forced landing
空难 air-crash
空中劫机 air piracy
劫机 hijack an airplane
乘机手续 check-in procedure
航班正点 flight regularity
航班不正点 flight irregularity
始发机场 departure airport
到达机场 arrival airport
安全检查 security check

success 成功

必备 经验 experience [ɪk'spɪərɪəns] *n.*
团队选择 team selection
目标 objective [əb'dʒektɪv] *n.*
性格 personality [ˌpɜːsə'nælətɪ] *n.*

乐观 optimism ['ɒptɪmɪzəm] *n.*
自信 confidence ['kɒnfɪdəns] *n.*
热情 enthusiasm [ɪn'θjuːzɪæzəm] *n.*
侵略性 aggressiveness [ə'gresɪvnɪs] *n.*
活力 energy ['enədʒɪ] *n.*
理想 ideal [aɪ'dɪəl] *n.*
积极态度 positive attitude
人际关系 personal relationship

theater 剧场

必备 主演 star [stɑː] *n.*
客串演出 guest appearance
成为明星 rise to stardom
拍外景 film on location
电影剧本 scenario [sɪ'nɑːriəʊ] *n.*
剪辑 edit ['edɪt] *n.*
字幕 caption ['kæpʃn]
字幕 subtitle ['sʌbtaɪtl] *n.*
解说 narration [nə'reɪʃn] *n.*
解说者 narrator [nə'reɪtə] *n.*
对话 dialogue ['daɪəlɒg] *n.*
超级明星 superstar ['suːpəstɑː] *n.*
淡出 fade out
淡入 fade in
特技画面 trick drawing
影帝 movie king
影后 movie queen
片名角色 title role
主角 leading role
男主角 hero ['hɪərəʊ] *n.*

男主角 leading man
女主角 heroine ['herəʊɪn] *n.*
女主角 leading lady
临时演员 film extra
替身 stand-in
特技演员 stunt man

选 记 剧院 theatre [θɪətə] *n.*
戏剧 drama ['drɑːmə] *n.*
喜剧 comedy ['kɒmɪdɪ] *n.*
悲剧 tragedy ['trædʒɪdɪ] *n.*
情节剧 melodrama ['melədrɑːmə] *n.*
哑剧 pantomime ['pæntəmaɪm] *n.*
首映 first night
首映 premiere ['premɪeə(r)] *n.*
开场白 prologue ['prəʊlɒg] *n.*
登场 entrance ['entrəns] *n.*
退场 exit ['egzɪt] *n.*
幕间休息 intermission [ˌɪntə'mɪʃən] *n.*
演出 performance [pə'fɔːməns] *n.*
排练 rehearsal [rɪ'hɜːsəl] *n.*
光圈 aperture ['æpətʃə(r)] *n.*
电影摄影机 cinecamera ['sɪnɪˌkæmərə] *n.*
目镜 eyepiece ['aɪpiːs] *n.*
滤光镜 filter ['fɪltə(r)] *n.*
快门 shutter ['ʃʌtə(r)] *n.*
取景器 viewfinder ['vjuːfaɪndə] *n.*
遮光罩 sunshade ['sʌnʃeɪd] *n.*
三角架 tripod ['traɪpɒd] *n.*
闪光灯 flashlight ['flæʃlaɪt] *n.*

片轴 spool [spuːl] *n.*

胶片，胶卷 film [fɪlm] *n.*

感光片 plate [pleɪt] *n.*

圆形剧场 amphitheatre [ˈæmfɪθɪətə] *n.*

舞台 stage [steɪdʒ] *n.*

舞台侧翼 wings [wɪŋz] *n.*

舞台道具 property [ˈprɒpətɪ] *n.*

脚灯 footlight [ˈfʊtlaɪt] *n.*

海报 poster [ˈpəʊstə] *n.*

节目单 program [ˈprəʊgræm] *n.*

保留节目 repertoire [ˈrepətwɑː(r)] *n.*

衣帽间 cloakroom [ˈkləʊkrʊm] *n.*

剧场休息厅 lounge [laʊndʒ] *n.*

包厢 box [bɒks] *n.*

引座员 usher [ˈʌʃə] *n.*

鼓掌 applause [əˈplɔːz] *n.*

喝彩 cheer [tʃɪə] *n.*

再来一个 encore [ɒŋˈkɔː] *n.*

剧作家 playwright [ˈpleɪraɪt] *n.*

小生 juvenile [ˈdʒuːvɪnaɪl] *n.*

试演 audition [ɔːˈdɪʃn] *n.*

丑角 clown [klaʊn] *n.*

售票处 box office

历史剧 historical play

独幕剧 one-act play

多幕剧 many-act play

音乐喜剧 musical comedy

肥皂剧 soap opera

彩排 dress rehearsal

预演 run-in
专场演出 special performance
巡回演出 road show
长期连演的戏 long-running play
剧名角色 title role
正面角色 positive role
配角 supporting role
男配角 male supporting role
女配角 female supporting role
次要角色 minor part
龙套角色 walking part
变换场景 transformation scene
谢幕 curtain call
谢幕礼 protocol of the curtain calls
最后一幕 drop scene
初排 walk-through
电视摄像机 television camera
广角镜头 wide-angle lens
变焦镜头 zoom lens
露天剧场 open-air theatre
中央剧场 arena theatre
实验剧场 experimental theatre
旋转舞台 revolving stage
中央舞台 theater-in-the-round
戏装 theatrical costume
舞台布置 stage setting
天幕 sky cloth
化妆室 dressing room
剧照 stage photo

艺名 stage name
票房 box office
招待票 privileged ticket
音乐会季票 concert season ticket
前排票 front row ticket
后排票 back row ticket
票根 ticket stub
戏票贩子 ticket tout
乐池 orchestra pit
安全门 emergency exit
戏院常客 theatre-goer
首场观众 first nighter
票友 amateur performer
戏迷 theatre fan
起立鼓掌 standing ovation
喝倒彩 make cat-calls
拍手喝倒彩 show handclap
戏剧评论家 stage critic
舞台演员 stage actor
舞台女演员 stage actress
舞台导演 stage director
剧中人物表 dramatic personae
舞台效果 stage effect
怯场 stage fright
冷场 stage-wait
京剧 Beijing opera
花脸 painted face type
武生 warrior role
武旦 female warrior role

电影制片厂 film studio
电影译制厂 film dubbing studio
把小说拍摄成电影 film a novel
拍电影 make a film
开始拍摄 start filming
试镜头 screen test

toy 玩具

必备 玩具娃娃 doll [dɒl] *n.*
芭比娃娃 Barbie ['bɑːbɪ] *n.*
绒毛玩具 stuffed animal
变形金刚 transformer [træns'fɔːmə] *n.*
泰迪熊 teddy bear
积木 magic cube
玩具枪 toy gun
开发他们的智力 develop their intelligence
给予玩具 afford toys
同玩具一起玩耍 play with toys
启发他们的理解力和才智 develop their wit and ability

transport 交通

Tips: 适用于关于交通的问题。例如：your favorite transport (你最喜爱的交通工具)、a vehicle you want to buy (你想买的车)。在描述城市、家乡时，也可以谈论此方面。

必备 品牌 brand [brænd] *n.*
安全 safety ['seɪftɪ] *n.*
郊区 suburb ['sʌbɜːb] *n.*
健康的 healthy ['helθɪ] *adj.*
车道 lane [leɪn] *n.*
消费者 consumer [kən'sjuːmə(r)] *n.*

行人 pedestrian [pɪ'destrɪən] *n.*
出口 exit ['eksɪt] *n.*
十字路口 crossing ['krɒsɪŋ] *n.*
停车 parking ['pɑːkɪŋ] *n.*
小偷 thief [θiːf] *n.*
经济型的 economical [ˌɪːkə'nɒmɪkəl] *adj.*
流线型的 streamlined ['striːmlaɪnd] *adj.*
音响系统 stereo system
黑色的车 black car
天窗 sunroof ['sʌnˌruːf] *n.*
享受阳光 enjoy the sunshine
底盘 chassis ['ʃæsɪ] *n.*
分期付款 on installment
交通堵塞 traffic jam
拥有一辆汽车 possess a car
对健康有益 beneficial to one's health
变得筋疲力尽 get exhausted
骑自行车 ride bicycles
骑自行车 ride a bike
锻炼手臂和腿部肌肉 exercise one's arm and leg muscles
修建更好的道路系统 build better road systems
汽车牌照 license plate
熟悉路线 familiar with the routes
驾驶技术 driving skill
对紧急情况的反应 respond to emergencies
对私有汽车征收重税 levy heavy tax on private cars
油价 oil price
保养车 maintain the car
道路建设 road construction

确保道路安全 ensure road safety
遵守交通规则 follow traffic rules
交通灯 traffic lights
在拐弯处放慢速度 slow down in turns
交通事故 traffic accidents
违反交通规则 violate the traffic rules
交通方式 means of transport
缺乏身体锻炼 lack physical exercise
忙碌的交通 busy traffic
保护环境 protect environment
制造污染 produce pollution
空气很闷 air is stuffy
私家车 private car
乘公共汽车 take the bus
公交车线路 bus route
高峰时间 rush hour
公路系统 road system
遵守交通规则 obey traffic rules
造成污染 cause pollution

travel 旅行

Tips: 适用于关于旅行的问题。例如：a journey / trip (一次旅行) 和 a place you want to go to (你想去的一个地方)。

必备 自然风景 natural beauty
名胜古迹 historical place
旅游业 tourism ['tʊərɪzəm] *n.*
旅程 itinerary [aɪ'tɪnərərɪ] *n.*
导游手册 guidebook ['gaɪdbʊk] *n.*
旅行目的地 destination [ˌdestɪ'neɪʃn] *n.*
旅行者 traveller ['trævələ(r)] *n.*

徒步旅行者 hiker ['haɪkə(r)] *n.*
海上旅行者 seafarer ['siːˌfeərə(r)] *n.*
集体旅行 excursion [ɪk'skɜːʃn] *n.*
短途旅游 outing ['aʊtɪŋ] *n.*
短途旅游 jaunt [dʒɔːnt] *n.*
远足 excursion [ɪk'skɜːʃn] *n.*
远足 go for an outing
蜜月旅行 honeymoon ['hʌnɪmuːn] *n.*
海上旅游 sea journey
海上观光 cruise [kruːz] *n.*
水上游览 voyage ['vɔɪɪdʒ] *n.*
徒步旅行 hike [haɪk] *n. & v.*
背包，徒步旅行背包 backpack ['bækpæk] *n.*
小型旅行手提箱 suitcase ['suːtkeɪs] *n.*
旅行壶 flask [flɑːsk] *n.*
太阳镜 sunglasses ['sʌnˌglɑːsɪz] *n.*
高空索道 ropeway ['rəʊpweɪ] *n.*
旅行社 travel agency
旅游服务 travel service
导游 tour guide
国际导游 guide interpreter
旅行证件 travel documents
旅游指南 travel brochure
游览图 tourist map
旅行支票 traveller's cheque
旅游护照 tourist card
旅游路线 tourist track
旅行距离 distance of travel
旅费 travelling expenses

旅游旺季 high season / tourist season
旅游淡季 out season
旅游萧条 tourist drought
旅游高峰时期 peak-travel period
游览来回票 excursion ticket
旅游纪念品 tourist souvenir
旅伴 travel companion
度假游客 holiday maker
观光团 tourist party
团体旅行 group travel
有导游的团体旅行 guided tour
自择旅游地的旅行 optional tour
豪华游 luxurious tour
经济游 economic tour
包餐旅游 inclusive tour
环球旅行 round-the-world tour
观光旅行 sightseeing tour
长途旅行 long journey
短途旅行 short journey
周末旅行 weekend trip
春游 spring outing
游山玩水 make a sightseeing tour
游园 visit a park or garden
游览飞行 sightseeing flight
乘车旅行 bus tour
旅行用品 travel kit
旅游服 outing dress
旅行鞋 hiking boots
登山鞋 mountaineering boots

睡袋 sleeping bag

急救箱 first-aid kit

缆车 cable car

景点门票 admission ticket

TV / radio program 电视 / 广播节目

Tips: 适用于 your favorite TV / radio program (最喜爱的电视或电台节目) 和 an interesting piece of news (一条有意思的新闻)。

必备 脱口秀 talk show

选秀节目 talent competition program

游戏类节目 game show

韩剧 Korean soaps

地方频道 local channel

电视主持人 TV presenter

知识丰富的 well-informed

让人们忘记学习或工作 distract people from study or work

选记 简明新闻 newsflash ['nju:zflæʃ] *n.*

特别节目 special ['speʃəl] *n.*

连播节目 serial ['sɪərɪəl] *n.*

电视连续剧 soaps [səʊps] *n.*

收视率 rating ['reɪtɪŋ] *n.*

暴力 violence ['vaɪələns] *n.*

误导的 misleading [ˌmɪs'li:dɪŋ] *adj.*

正直 integrity [ɪn'tegrətɪ] *n.*

导播 director [dɪ'rektə(r)] *n.*

电台 radio station

电视台 television station

国内新闻 home news

国际新闻 international news

世界新闻 world news

新闻提要 news headlines
新闻概要 news summary
新闻报道 news report
新闻简报 news bulletin
早晨新闻 morning news
晚间新闻 evening news
经济新闻 economic news
实况广播节目 live programme
娱乐性节目 light programme
采访节目 interview programme
音乐节目 music programme
音乐节目录像 music video
英语节目 English programme
教育节目 educational programme
现场直播讨论节目 talk-in
访谈节目 chat show / talk show
联播节目 network show
商业节目 commercial programme
观众来电直播节目 phone-in / call-in
广播谈话 radio talk
智力竞赛节目 quiz show
天气预报 weather forecast
气象报告 weather report
点播节目 request programme
广播剧 radio play
电视片 video film
广播评论 broadcast commentary
新闻报道度 news coverage
虚假新闻 false news
责任感 sense of responsibility

type of music 音乐种类

必备 歌剧 opera ['ɒpərə] *n.*
交响曲 symphony ['sɪmfənɪ] *n.*
协奏曲 concerto [kən'tʃɜːtəʊ] *n.*
奏鸣曲 sonata [sə'nɑːtə] *n.*
华尔兹 waltz [wɔːls] *n.*
小夜曲 serenade [ˌserə'neɪd] *n.*
进行曲 march [mɑːtʃ] *n.*
布鲁斯 blues [bluːz] *n.*
歌 song [sɒŋ] *n.*
旋律 melody ['melədɪ] *n.*
曲调 tune [tjuːn] *n.*
传统的 traditional [trə'dɪʃənl] *adj.*
手风琴 accordion [ə'kɔːdɪən] *n.*
萨克斯管 saxophone ['sæksəfəʊn] *n.*
小号 trumpet ['trʌmpɪt] *n.*
鼓 drum [drʌm] *n.*
木琴 xylophone ['zaɪləfəʊn] *n.*
大提琴 cello ['tʃeləʊ] *n.*
主题 theme [θiːm] *n.*
小溪 brook [brʊk] *n.*
优雅的，高雅的 elegant ['elɪgənt] *adj.*
情感的 emotional [ɪ'məʊʃənl] *adj.*
抒情的 lyrics ['lɪrɪks] *adj.*
分散 distract [dɪ'strækt] *v.*
校园 campus ['kæmpəs] *n.*
曲调 melody ['melədɪ] *n.*
保守的 conservative [kən'sɜːvətɪv] *adj.*
音乐节 music festival

古典音乐 classical music
教会音乐 church music
轻音乐 light music
器乐 instrumental music
声乐 vocal music
室内乐 chamber music
爵士乐 jazz music
乡村音乐 country music
摇滚乐 rock and roll
流行歌曲 pop song
民歌 folk song
艺术歌曲 art song
民乐 folk music
古乐 ancient music
做甜美的梦 have a sweet dream
嘻哈音乐 hip-hop
流行音乐 pop music
传统戏剧 traditional operas
弹乐器 play instruments
鉴赏音乐 appreciate music
吹笛子 play the flute
感到孤独或者有压力 feel lonely or stressful
一种消遣的方式 a way of relaxation
弹钢琴 play the piano
在卡拉OK唱歌 sing the karaoke
喜欢流行 enjoy popularity
学业学习 academic study
中国音乐 Chinese music
西方音乐 western music
现场演出 live show

water resource 水资源

选记 海 sea [siː] *n.*

大洋 ocean ['əʊʃn] *n.*

海湾 bay [beɪ] *n.*

海湾 gulf [gʌlf] *n.*

湾 cove [kəʊv] *n.*

海角 cape [keɪp] *n.*

悬崖 cliff [klɪf] *n.*

港 port [pɔːt] *n.*

港 harbour ['hɑːbə(r)] *n.*

海滩 beach [biːtʃ] *n.*

海峡 strait [streɪt] *n.*

地峡 isthmus ['ɪsməs] *n.*

礁石 reef [riːf] *n.*

暗礁 key [kiː] *n.*

沙洲 sandbar ['sændbɑː(r)] *n.*

潮 tide [taɪd] *n.*

浪 wave [weɪv] *n.*

风暴 tempest ['tempɪst] *n.*

海震 seaquake ['siːkweɪk] *n.*

冰山 iceberg ['aɪsbɜːg] *n.*

海岸 shore [ʃɔː(r)] *n.*

湖港区 estuary ['estʃʊərɪ] *n.*

三角洲 delta ['deltə] *n.*

水流 current ['kʌrənt] *n.*

小溪 stream [striːm] *n.*

小溪 brook [brʊk] *n.*

湍流山溪 torrent ['tɒrənt] *n.*

泉 spring [sprɪŋ] *n.*

河床 bed [bed] *n.*
瀑布 waterfall ['wɔːtəfɔːl] *n.*
大瀑布 cataract ['kætərækt] *n.*
支流 tributary ['trɪbjətrɪ] *n.*
运河 canal [kə'næl] *n.*
远海 high seas / open seas
领海 territorial water
高原湖泊 plateau lake
美丽风景 beautiful scenery
篝火晚会 bonfire party
明亮的阳光 bright sunshine
拾果子 pick fresh fruit
冲浪 go surfing
划船 go boating
打水球 play water polo
划独木舟 go canoeing
滑水 go water skiing
水资源 water resource
水面 surface of water
倾倒废水 dump waste water
流经 flow through

weather 天气

Tips: 适用于关于天气的问题。在描述城市、家乡时，可以提及天气的内容。

必备 寒冷的 chilly ['tʃɪlɪ] *adj.*
霜冻 frost [frɒst] *n.*
冰冷的 icy ['aɪsɪ] *adj.*
雨夹雪 sleet [sliːt] *n.*
暴风雪 blizzards ['blɪzədz] *n.*

雪堆 snowdrift ['snəʊdrɪft] *n.*
融化 melt [melt] *v.*
透不过气的 stifling ['staɪflɪŋ] *adj.*
潮湿的 humid ['hjuːmɪd] *adj.*
潮湿的 damp [dæmp] *adj.*
燥热的 scorching ['skɔːtʃɪŋ] *adj.*
燥热的 boiling ['bɔɪlɪŋ] *adj.*
温和的 mild [maɪld] *adj.*
毛毛雨 drizzle ['drɪzl] *n.*
大雾 thick fog

选记 易变的 changeable ['tʃeɪndʒəbl] *adj.*
破坏 destroy [dɪ'strɔɪ] *v.*
地震 earthquake ['ɜːθkweɪk] *n.*
洪水 flood [flʌd] *n.*
伤亡 casualty ['kæʒʊəltɪ] *n.*
强风 strong wind
影响心情 affect mood
发脾气 lose temper
引起房屋和财产的破坏 cause damage to houses and property
减小灾难的影响 minimize bad effects of disasters
精确的天气预报 accurate weather forecast
采取预防措施 take precautions

website 网站

必备 提供娱乐 provide sb. with entertainment
联系人们 connect people
玩网络游戏 play online games
上网 surf the Internet
网上购物 do online shopping

wedding 婚礼

Tips: 适用于 a wedding（一次婚礼）。

必备 同事 colleague ['kɒliːg] *n.*
新娘 bride [braɪd] *n.*
新郎 bridegroom ['braɪdgruːm] *n.*
伴郎 bestman ['bestmən] *n.*
伴娘 bridesmaid ['braɪdzmeɪd] *n.*
新娘捧花 bouquet [bʊ'keɪ] *n.*
敬酒 toast [təʊst] *n.*
客人 guest [gest] *n.*
表现 perform [pə'fɔːm] *v.*
婚姻 marriage ['mærɪdʒ] *n.*
装饰 decoration [ˌdekə'reɪʃn] *n.*
气氛 atmosphere ['ætməsfɪə(r)] *n.*
告别 farewell [feə'wel] *n.*
婚礼 wedding ceremony
婚纱 wedding dress
拜天地 pay homege to heaven and earth
喝彩和掌声 cheer and clap

weekend 周末

必备 跑跑卡丁车 popkart ['pɒpkɑːt] *n.*
空闲时间 free time
闲暇时间 leisure time
去健身房 go to gym
外出就餐 have dinner out
看韩剧 watch Korean soaps
读在线小说 read novels online
打游戏 play online games
魔兽世界 World of Warcraft

做家务 do the housework

玩联众游戏 play games on Mygame